ADRIE DOLMAN

AGILE COACHING

THE DUTCH WAY

Copyright: © Adapt2Value B.V. & Adrie Dolman, 2021
Cover: Adept, Velserbroek
Inside work: Pre Press Media Groep, Zeist
Editorial office: Fleur van Goppel (Dutch version)
Translation: Natalie Bowler-Geerinck
ISBN: 978 90 903 4083 8
NUR: 808

PREFACE

***How to help organizations
discover ways to deliver
the highest value
in the shortest time and with the least risk***

With the current dire shortage of real agile coaches, we need more than just superficial knowledge – we need experts. Many books merely describe agile theory, methods, and processes but for a successful agile coach, having a mental model of their own is crucial.

Successful agile coaches see the organization as a system and assume the role of a system developer. They facilitate an organic process that breaks through old patterns, paving the way for the agile organization. All this is done according to the system approach, built up based on the mental model and the meaning assigned to it by the people who are part of the system.

This book does not purport to change you and prescribe what you should or should not do. This book describes in detail the beliefs and steps with which you can become a successful agile coach, while staying true to yourself.

I hope you enjoy reading this book!
Adrie Dolman MSc

Preface Ahmed Sidky (Los Angeles Metropolitan Area, USA)

Adrie Dolman's book is a true gift to the agile coaching community. Years of insights and experiences coaching individuals, teams, and organizations are curated into this amazing book. There are countless practical tips, tricks, learnings, models, and tools that will enhance any agile coach and accelerate their growth and skill development.

Adrie's focus on Agile as a mindset and how to coach to that mindset is brilliant.

This book is truly a great addition to any Agile coach's library. If you are an aspiring agile coach this is a must-read.

Ahmed Sidky, Ph.D.
President of the International Consortium for Agile (ICAgile)
Head of Business Agility at Riot Games

Preface Andrea Fryrear (Colorado, USA)

There are no shortage of resources on Agile coaching in the world, but many of them assume that you're doing two things: developing software and using Scrum exclusively. What Adrie has created here, however, is a deeply practical guide for any and all Agile coaches, leaving such unhelpful assumptions at the door.

Adrie is diligent in avoiding prescription and leaning into description, but I can guarantee that the following pages will nonetheless be enormously practical for agilists looking to build up their coaching capabilities. Despite having spent many years of my own in the trenches working with Agile marketing teams, I found myself highlighting entire sections for reference. I'm already looking forward to sharing the illuminating charts and diagrams with my own team of coaches to help guide their individual growth.

And yet this book isn't just a simple how-to or a compilation of exercises. Adrie shows us the full arc of Agile's evolution, tracing its origins far beyond twentieth-

century software development and back into the minds of pioneers of the scientific method hundreds of years ago. He skillfully connects this history to how coaches need to show up for their teams, freeing them from dogmatic adherence to practices that may or may not apply to the kinds of work their teams are doing.

From Francis Bacon to Steve Denning, Adrie deftly tracks how Agile came to be the defining method for getting stuff done in the twenty-first century. What's more, he plucks out important takeaways from all its phases to guide Agile coaches whose working life is far more complex, uncertain, and ambiguous than the one Bacon found himself in.

Being an Agile coach is one of the most severely challenging and deeply rewarding jobs on the planet. Sometimes it feels like both of those things in the course of a single meeting. At times being an Agile coach is akin to trudging through the desert with no supplies, trying to reach an uncertain destination while herding a reluctant pack of cats. Resources like this one are an oasis on this difficult journey.

If you're an experienced Agile coach, rejoice. Here's a careful, considerate fellow practitioner who's opening his toolkit to share ideas with you.

If you're looking to start on your Agile coaching journey, great news. Someone who's spent years traversing that path has come back to offer guidance.

Agile coaches of all kinds will find value in these pages. For those, like me, who spend our days bringing Agile outside the realms of software development or IT, you won't encounter overwhelming references to releases, demos, bugs, or code bases. Anyone who tries to nurture the Agile mindset and its corresponding ways of working should stop messing around with my introduction, and dig into this outstanding resource right away.

Andrea Fryrear
Agile Marketing Coach & Trainer, Co-Founder AgileSherpas

Preface Michael K Sahota (North York, Canada)

When Adrie Dolman reached out to me to see if I would write a foreword, I wondered to myself: Who is this guy? How can he contribute to such a crowded field? How does his work relate to the work I am bringing to the world? Agile Coaching is a complex, broad topic: there are many valuable, distinct and even contradictory views.

What this book delivers is a practical, human in-the-trenches view of what it takes day in and day out to operate as an agent of change. The book is full of many useful tools and models that will help anyone aspiring to be an effective Agile Coach.

The part of the book that resonated the most with my own views is the importance of your own development. He says "Your most important tool is you, and you have to master that tool properly before you start using it." This is a point that often gets missed and is actually the foundation of one's effectiveness.

What may happen as you dive into the practices of this book is that you discover your own leadership and how to make local change to culture without talking about it. My hope for you is that you begin to model the shift of what Agile is really all about.

I hope you enjoy it.

Michael K Sahota
Certified Enterprise Coach, Author, Trainer and Consultant

Preface John Cass (Washington, USA)

In 2008 when I became aware of agile for marketers, the Dutch were ahead of the curve with the practice. So I was excited to learn when Adrie Dolman had written his new book "Agile Coaching - The Dutch Way".

His book is all about how agile coaches approach agile coaching. This book is a how-to for coaches. What stood out for me was the thorough review of how to become an agile coach for an organization; from maturity models, to toolboxes, to personal insights from Adrie on what to expect. Great stuff for team members wanting to become an agile coach the Dutch way!

John Cass
Organizer, Boston Agile Marketing Meetup
Podcaster, A Deep Dive into Agile Marketing with John Cass

Preface André Felippa, (Sao Paulo, Brazil)

Do you aspire to become an Agile Coach? Or maybe you are already an experienced agilist looking for new inspiration, examples and practical tools?

For a long time I've been searching for great practical recommendations for Agile Coaches like myself. And there are already plenty of books in the market which cover the Agile frameworks, team-forming and scaling-up, but Adrie's book is quite unique.

Adrie skillfully draws from his own extensive coaching experience to offer us a structured pathway to become a great Agile Coach, covering all aspects of this delightful job, whilst also sharing a wealth of helpful and practical examples, tools and techniques, which can easily inspire and be applied by any agile enthusiast, regardless of your own agile maturity level.

I hope that you may enjoy the reading and extract as much value from this great book as I did.

André Felippa
C-Level Agile Coach and MD at Adventures Inc. / Brazil

Evan Leybourn (Victoria, Australia)

At the time of writing this preface, the Agile Manifesto is just about to turn 20 years old. And yet, as Adrie makes clear in his book, agility is much older than that. This is nowhere clearer than in Æsop's Fables, a collection of stories and fables from ancient Greece over 2500 years ago (between 620–564 BCE). Let me share with you the fable of the Oak and the Reed (translated by George Fyler Townsend in 1887).

A very large Oak was uprooted by the wind and thrown across a stream. It fell among some Reeds, which it thus addressed: "I wonder how you, who are so light and weak, are not entirely crushed by these strong winds." They replied, "You fight and contend with the wind, and consequently you are destroyed; while we on the contrary bend before the least breath of air, and therefore remain unbroken, and escape."

This remains one of the best descriptions of agility today. So the question must be asked, if agility has been valued for millennia, why is it that we have so many Oaks in modern business? The simple answer is that agility is harder to achieve and maintain than rigidity; and when the winds are calm no one values agility. But, to extend the metaphor, the winds aren't calm. Just take a look back at the last decade, from 2010 to 2020, to see how volatile and unpredictable the world we live in is.

Which is where agile coaching comes in. Whether in a marketing team, product development, or across an entire organization, agile coaching helps people who aspire to agility, achieve it. And for any aspiring coach, Adrie's book is a must-read, and practical, guide to the craft.

Evan Leybourn
CEO, Business Agility Institute

CONTENT

WHY IS AGILE COACHING IMPORTANT?

We live in a VUCA world: **V**olatility, **U**ncertainty, **C**omplexity, and **A**mbiguity. In other words, the world today is becoming increasingly turbulent, unstable and vague. Organizations are taking a radical turn in their search for a system that can easily adapt to rapid changes. Agility is one such system. It is not hype – agile is the new lifeline.

People want to matter and be of value. They want to develop and be a part of something that they can be proud of. People derive their self-esteem from a winning sports club, a volunteer organization, a happy family or a promising company, for example.

Agile Coaching gives new meaning to organizations and people in the VUCA world. It serves as the basis for an organic company culture, an inspiring team spirit, and healthy, motivated people. This cannot be achieved by just calling something agile (Agile In Name Only) or encouraging your teams to scrum without an agile mindset. The environment in which the agile team operates must actually be agile, and the team and the mindset of the team members should also be purely agile. This requires, or rather demands, real agile coaching, much more and much better than the current average. The people who demonstrate they are capable of top-level performance with an agile mindset are still very much the large minority. The longer the rest continues to lag behind, the higher the market share that the handful of agile purists will have thrown into their lap. This brings unwanted inequality into the world, and unnecessarily so. In my opinion, the majority of organizations should be able to add high value to the market. Not only would this make these organizations more pleasant, profitable and valuable, it would also contribute to equality in our society and happiness for many.

Why would you want to be an agile coach?

If it frustrates you that organizations in our current VUCA climate are holding themselves back and thus undermining their future prospects. And if you get a kick out of helping the people in those organizations emerge from their paralysis of old thinking patterns, so that they can deliver the highest value in the market. Then you are probably an agile coach or want to become one. Or maybe you are an entrepreneur, interim manager, troubleshooter, company doctor, consultant, trainer, speaker or manager with an agile mindset, and you act like an agile coach. Confused? In the course of this book, you will come to understand that there are more agile coaches than people who call themselves agile coaches. And that there are people who call themselves agile coach but aren't in reality. What organizations need are real agile coaches, lots of real agile coaches. I hope you are one or want to become one. You will make the world a little bit better.

If you look with different eyes, you see new things

Every change or improvement starts with a different way of looking: different from how it is generally viewed. If you want to develop a better car, you should not look at the current cars with their current standards. It helps to start by looking at the users of cars differently, to really understand their needs, and then to think about how you can make a better car.

This is the line I follow in this book. I always want to approach the topics based on the mental model. In other words, how does an agile coach look at this? Based on which interpretation, knowledge, and belief? My expectation is that the people who read this book are also able to look at things in a different way. Next, I describe how an agile coach deals with this in practice.

Many things about agile and agile working are unclear. You may have adopted a prevailing view, which is not always useful when you want to become or be a good agile coach. That is why on the following pages I will first introduce some common misconceptions about agile. This will help you to re-interpret several confusing words and ways of thinking.

LOOKING BASED ON A BETTER UNDERSTANDING

Agile is more than 400 years old

Many people think that agile was invented in the IT sector. Many books that write a few lines about agile even say so outright. But this is not true. Agility as a scientific method is actually 400 years old and has its origins in 1620. The method was inspired by the Italian physicist, astronomer, mathematician and philosopher Galileo Galilei, and established by scientific pioneer Francis Bacon. The latter is also known as the father of empiricism. Bacon argued that researchers should be like small children, and that the best way to learn from observed facts is through experimentation and observation. His dedication likely resulted in his death: he died of pneumonia in 1626 while studying the effects of freezing meat on its shelf life.

In the nineteenth and twentieth centuries, the method was enriched from various scientific sides with pragmatism and refined empiricism, creating a practically usable empirical cycle that we still use today, albeit in an improved form:

1. Collect facts based on observation.
2. Based on the facts, develop a general theory that explains the facts.
3. Translate the theory into a prediction in the form of a specifically formulated and verifiable hypothesis.
4. Conduct an experiment to test the hypothesis, following which you can confirm or reject the hypothesis.
5. From here, the cycle starts again.

In the twentieth century, Darwinism and the '80-20 rule' further fueled, optimized, and finetuned the agile approach. The naturalist Charles Darwin, world famous for his theory of evolution, discovered in the 19th century that your chances of survival increase more with well-functioning adaptive ability than with intelligence or power. This fact is clearly reflected in the agile principles as described further on in this book. And if you can learn as much from 20% as you can from 100%, you can go five times faster or deliver much more value in the same time. Of course, you will need to find a way to determine which 20% to choose. In 1930, Walter Steward used the PDSA cycle (Plan-Do-Study-Act, later renamed by William Edwards Deming as the PDCA: Plan-Do-Check-Act quality circle) to improve products and processes. After that, things progressed rapidly and scientific discoveries and best practices followed each other quickly. Steve Blank then taught us to make the link between truly understanding customers' or users' deepest motivations and developing valuable products. Dave Snowden demonstrated that complex environments thrive the most in a self-organizing adaptive system. Robert K. Greenleaf established that Servant Leadership yields more than bosses with big egos. Taiichi Ohno taught us about the seven biggest wastes. Steve Denning made us aware that we can only move forward after a radical change in management thinking. Patrick Lencioni and Tuckman taught us how to develop high-performing teams. Eric Ries (Lean Start-Up) and Ash Maurya (Running Lean) brought the focus back to the importance of the business. This list is the cradle of everything we use today under the agile umbrella, such as Lean Start-up, Scrum, UX, Design Thinking, and many models that are all aimed at learning and deciding faster and better.

It appears the urge to win is strong. In wars, people want to win from the enemy, and in business from the competition. The agile approach popped up wherever environments were unpredictable, and rapid adaptation to the new or future reality proved necessary in order to win or survive.

Barry Boehm showed in 1986 and 1988 that development processes are most effective when we consciously allow errors to occur at the beginning. This view is particularly popular among agilists and is better known as 'fail fast!'. This approach ensures that failure and repair costs are kept to a minimum, and sufficient time and budget are left to work on the highest value in a focused manner. To this end, he developed the spiral model for prototyping: the basis of the current step-by-step agile approach for incremental development.

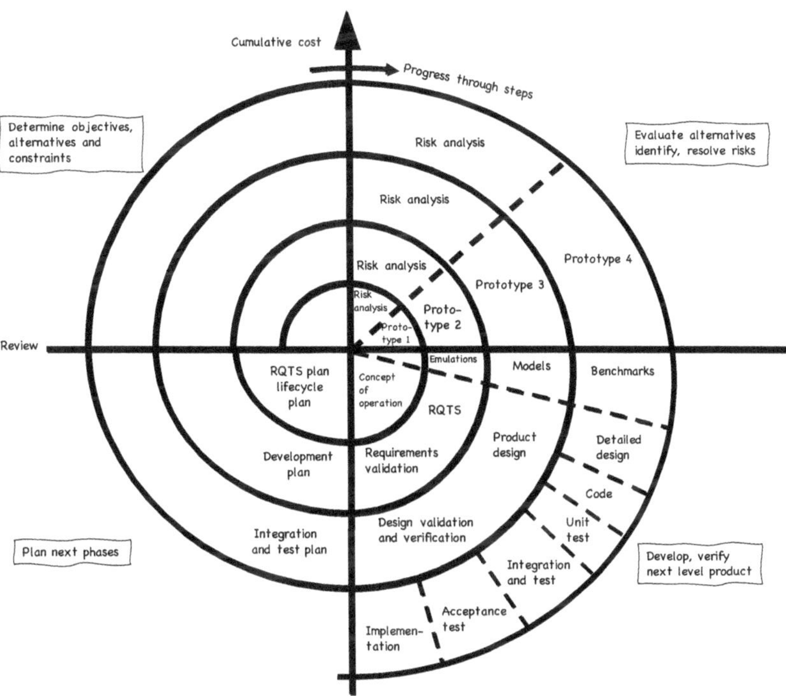

In 1986, Takeuchie, a professor of strategy at Harvard University, and co-author Nonaka published their groundbreaking article on The New New Product Development Game. It described how certain manufacturers innovated faster and more successfully than their competitors. They identified a kind of team approach that was not unlike that of a rugby team. It turned out the approach was based on many experiments and observations from the business world, and on wisdom from Taoism. By thinking entirely freely and through empirical validation, they developed new patterns, which are now enthusiastically welcomed all over the world. Organizations such as Google, Amazon and Tesla are set up according to this agile mindset and are growing rapidly. Apple and General Electric owe it their survival. If they had not been transformed into an agile organization with a focus on value rather than on technology or products, they would probably have vanished from the market.

Many people mistakenly hold on to the static predictability or malleability of things. Taoism was originally a strict ethical philosophy about the meaning of our existence and how we can do the right thing. According to Taoism, everything is in perfect harmony when there is constant change. The balance changes all the time, and nothing can exist without its opposite. Yin and Yang is the infinite and fundamental principle of evolution and self-organization. These are excellent guidelines for good leadership in the current zeitgeist, where change is the only constant factor.

In IT, many things went wrong in the 1990s. IT projects would overrun almost as a matter of course and regularly delivered insufficient or no value for users. At the time, financiers even assumed that if an IT project was estimated at ten million, it would end up costing thirty million. This rather absurd calculation standard was a harsh reality at the time. The Dutch government alone wasted five billion euros on IT projects every year. This went on for many years, all over the world. The need to replace the waterfall method that was popular at the time was obviously pressing. The waterfall method is based on predictability as we came to know it during the industrial age. This has turned out to be a myth, however, in software development – unless you can predict the future with a crystal ball, of course, but that has now also been scientifically undermined. You will only know whether software does what it should do when you give it to a user. Until then, everything you develop is a mere assumption. It follows that if you draw up an extensive and detailed plan in advance to which everyone has to adhere, adjusting becomes more difficult and the chances of creating a successful product are reduced.

A search among universities to find a suitable vision and approach for IT projects yielded the scientific basis for an agile vision and working method. Ken Schwaber and Jeff Sutherland adopted the agile mindset in their daily work and, based on their findings, came up with the first step toward an agile framework for software development. The framework was to provide guidance for agile development teams, with sufficient space to tailor it to their own situation. They dubbed their framework Scrum, inspired by The New New Product Development Game. It drew a comparison with rugby teams, that also use this term for 'regularly putting their heads together and then all going for a try together'. In other words, agile and scrum are not the same thing. Agile is something you are, while scrum is something you do. If you scrum, that does not necessarily mean that you are agile. But if you are agile, scrum is actually very useful. As a framework, it offers a fantastic handle for development teams that are agile. You could see scrum as a set of rules that helps the team work together in an agile way. Incidentally, you can also be very agile without scrumming.

Agile thinking is still developing. It continues to increase its value as more and more organizations learn to grasp and apply its essence.

A better understanding of software

Software is not necessarily related to IT. Soft means something that is not yet 'hard'. For example, there may be some uncertainty about the what or how. Or it may be something that is constantly in development, for example, because otherwise it would lose its value. People, for example, are physically hard: a surgeon knows exactly where to cut when he starts to operate, and this will not have changed next month. Mentally, however, people are soft: a coach will need to delve time and again into someone's mood and into the beliefs through which the coachee is now looking at the world. Our body is the hardware, the mental part of us is the software.

A better understanding of a system

A (software) system is an orderly collection of related elements with mutual relationships that are aimed at a common goal. The elements interact with each other. In this context, organizations are systems too, in which the achievement of a common goal is realized through the interaction between the different elements. The organization as a system is subject to evolution and continuous development; it is never finished. This is the type of environment where agile thrives.

A better understanding of value

Value does not mean the turnover or the profit that your work produces. Nor is it about cuts or savings. Value is the benefit to a buyer or user for which they are willing to pay or make an effort. The definition of value to the customer can be illustrated as follows.

$$\text{Value for the customer} = \frac{\text{Product} + \text{Experience}}{\text{Price} + \text{Effort}}$$

Turnover and profit do not lead to value for the customer. Conversely, value for the customer does lead to turnover and profit. So, the more valuable something is to a buyer or user, the more turnover and profit it will bring you. It follows that focusing on value creation for the user yields more turnover and profit than focusing on turnover and profit. Despite the fact that Steve Denning had already scientifically substantiated this premise in the 20th century with his Radical Management theory, many companies still manage directly for turnover and profit – with all the consequences this entails. They are not exactly the most profitable companies, and they are probably no longer growing. And anything that is not growing, is slowly but surely dying. This is a law of economics that knows no mercy.

A better understanding of growth

The previous paragraph also calls for a better interpretation of the concept of growth. Many companies think of growth in terms of turnover, profit, or the number of employees. In the agile world, growth means learning more and becoming smarter. You grow in terms of knowledge and skills. Again, having more turnover, profit, or employees does not mean that you learn more and become smarter. But if you learn more and become smarter, you can increase your turnover and profit.

A better understanding of a product

Within agile, 'product' does not mean the tangible product. The product is the value driver: it ensures that the customer or user receives the value. For example, facilitating a good dialogue is one of the most important products a coach can offer. And coaches can distinguish themselves by using different working methods and thus offering a better dialogue than their competitors do. Customers do not buy products, but rather the value that these products yield for them. Emotional value, or the product experience, is usually the highest value. As soon as another value driver is better able to deliver emotional value to the customer, your product stops offering value to the customer or user. When this happens, your product ceases to be relevant.

A better understanding of quality

Now that we have a better understanding of value and a product, it is interesting to also further examine the concept of quality. Quality means meeting expectations. You can describe this in a formula: $Q = Ee - En$ (Quality = Experience minus Expectation). This means it is a relative concept, and highly personal. What is more, it changes over time. In the past, one would expect a bank to provide you with a clear and comprehensible paper bank statement by post every fortnight. If a bank met this expectation, it would have delivered good quality. Nowadays, most people expect to be able to view their bank transactions and balance in real time on their smartphones. If the bank now sends a bank statement, most people will experience this as a waste of paper and ink. That very same statement is no longer considered to offer quality. This is how quality evolves over time. From paid Wi-Fi to free Wi-Fi, from limited opening hours to 24/7, from queueing at the cashier's to self-scan, from login code to facial recognition, from course to blended learning and from combustion engine to electric car.

A better understanding of the highest goal in agile

These days, simply meeting customer expectations is no longer enough – customers take this for granted. And if you get it wrong once, it quickly becomes a dissatisfier: an immediate reason to be dissatisfied and potentially switch to a different product or supplier.

Customers choose products and suppliers that exceed customer expectations. If the value of a product exceeds customer expectations, this triggers emotional reactions from customers, with the result that they enthusiastically start talking about this with other customers. This peer-to-peer excitement works like a magnet and gives organizations the most sustainable right to exist. The highest goal in the agile organization is to continuously surprise customers with values that they did not ask for, but that enthuse them. One example is the "Anything for a smile' campaign by Dutch e-commerce company Coolblue. Customers will only flash that smile when you exceed their expectations with something they perceive as valuable. Coolblue challenges all its employees to come up with something new every day, so that they can exceed Coolblue's new customer expectations.

A better understanding of games

Many coaches use games to facilitate the desired dialogue. They may suggest games as a fun way to while away the time, but games are a working method that challenges participants. A game has a clear goal, it describes the context and provides rules for how the participants deal with it. Games can be used to diverge, for example, to come up with as many new ideas as possible for a cool feature. They can also be used to converge, to distill just one or a few ideas, which creates focus and starts the validation process. Games also lend themselves to an initial rough pre-validation among users, particularly when there is no practice in which to test yet. In a fictional setting, participants show through their behavior what they would never say in words. The agile coach observes what happens during the games. Where is the emotion? Where are the hidden obstacles in the thinking process? And where are the opportunities to further develop this team's thinking toward an agile mindset?

Games are very powerful as a working method. As a father, I worry that my thirteen-year-old son is more interested in online gaming than in the rest of the world. This is because game developers consciously let the participants enter at a low level and challenge them to reach the 'next level'. In this way, participants experience that they are able to win and to keep getting better. They are rewarded for doing so, and allowed to proceed to a higher level. I have noticed in my son that this can become addictive. There is no point in fighting it; at best I can try to compete with the games by letting my son discover that he is capable of winning in other areas, getting rewards and recognition for this, and proceeding to a higher level. So far, I don't have the impression that his school can compete with online gaming, although a school should have all the ingredients to do so. That is why I regularly take my son mountain-biking in the woods. Whenever I notice that he is ready to handle more, we choose a more challenging course or a longer distance. And I invest in him with new clothes, a better bike, my compliments, and explicit recognition by expressing my admiration for him in front of other people. Challenging and rewarding a person in this way brings the participant into the flow channel. The participant is continuously challenged at their own level and receives rewards for this, which creates recognition and the experience that they can grow, and are growing, a lot. This is what makes games attractive. In a work or coaching situation, the same applies; I will come back to this later.

A better understanding of pain

Pain is where improvement is possible: often unmet needs that organizations fail to address because they cannot oversee the impact. Fearing that they might lose, they accept the pain and put off solving a problem or making a change. This does not mean that the organization (currently) experiences this as pain. Most pain is not experienced by realizing that you run the risk of having an accident. You do not experience the pain until you have had the accident. The same is true for many organizations. As long as we can get away with it, we don't believe the accident will happen to us. And when the accident does happen to us, we blame others. An agile coach identifies the potential pain faster than the organization, because as an outsider he is more alert to it. He will start working on this before the organization experiences the pain. In my experience, there are no pain-free organizations; every organization can do better.

How to read this book?

In this book, you will regularly read about a bit of 'pain'. I will explain this pain with examples from science or contemporary facts. Next, I will consider the case through agile glasses and describe how I think we can treat this pain. As a result, the book is sometimes partly subjective, because I describe the approach based on my personal experience. It is impossible to describe every variant, because every practical situation is different and has thousands of variables. The context will never be quite the same, although the principles based on which an agile coach works are.

And while we're on the subject of how to read this book: wherever I refer to someone as 'he', you can, of course, also read 'she'. And vice versa. There are many fantastic male and female agile coaches, managers, directors, Product Owners, Scrum Masters and team members.

BASIC KNOWLEDGE FOR ANYONE WHO WANTS TO BECOME AN AGILE COACH

Agile is a mindset. It is the mental model of one or more people who believe that adapting swiftly to the changing environment will result in improvement. It is the belief that even if you cannot change the wind, you can change the position of your sails. In other words, you cannot change the world, but you can change yourself, to alter the effects of the changing world. Agile is primarily about who you are and why you do things. Next, you can consider what you do or how you do it. If something changes in the environment (world, industry, etc.), you won't feel the need to complain about the world. Instead, you will feel a rush of energy and the desire to adapt to the new situation as quickly as possible – in a way that maintains your value or even increases it. It is all about your belief that learning and changing can be done much faster, with less risk of waste and more value as a result.

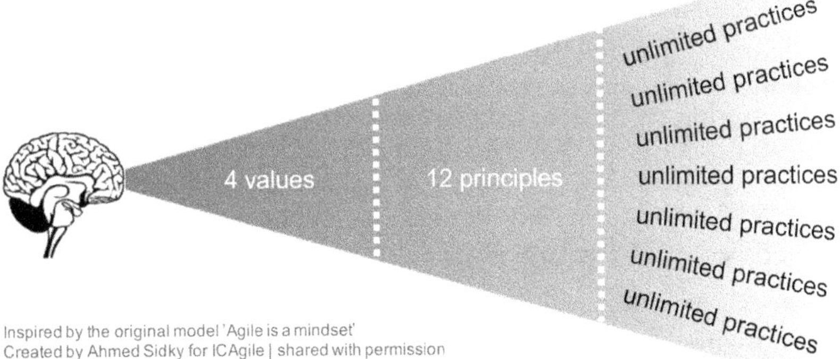

Inspired by the original model 'Agile is a mindset'
Created by Ahmed Sidky for ICAgile | shared with permission

In other words, agile is not a method or a project management approach. It is a belief in certain values and principles that lead to improved ways to develop value. An agile mindset offers guidance to turn innovative development processes into a success. The pitfall of adopting a fixed method or project management approach is obvious, but it will only be effective as long as it is carried with an agile mindset.

In order to make agile ideas shareable, a group of seventeen entrepreneurs and developers summarized this in an Agile Manifesto in 2001, at a meeting in Utah. Below is a free interpretation.

Agile development values

1. We value individuals and their interactions more than processes and tools.
2. We value working products more than extensive documentation.
3. We value working with our customer or user more than contract negotiations.
4. We value responding to changes more than following a plan.

This isn't to say that there is no value in processes, tools, documentation, contract negotiations, and following a plan. However, we are often so busy with this that we forget that people are much more effective if they prioritize the professionals and how they interact, focus on a working product (however small), collaborate with customers or users and respond more quickly to changes. In other words: focus on what really makes the difference.

Agile development principles

1. Our highest priority is to surprise our customer or user by delivering valuable products quickly and continuously.

2. We welcome change, even when it happens late in the development process. It is precisely thanks to these changes that the agile working method offers a competitive advantage.
3. We continue to supply valuable products or product features frequently, ranging from every few weeks to every few months, with a preference for the shortest interval.
4. Business and IT work together on their value creation in development teams on a daily basis.
5. We develop new values with motivated professionals. We give them the space and support they need. We trust them to deliver the highest possible value.
6. The most efficient and effective way to share information with or within a development team is a face-to-face conversation.
7. A working product is the primary way to measure progress.
8. Agile processes promote sustainable development. The sponsors, developers and users must be able to indefinitely maintain a constant pace.
9. Continuous attention to technical excellence and good design increase agility.
10. Simplicity – the art of maximizing the amount of work we don't do – is essential.
11. The best architecture, requirements and designs are created in self-organizing teams.
12. The team regularly reflects on how it can increase effectiveness, and adjusts its behavior accordingly.

This manifesto is available online (agilemanifesto.org) and can be consulted in 68 languages.

In short, you could say that we believe in highly skilled professionals who, in self-organization, continuously (as first in the market) surprise their customers with new values. They do not follow the change, they are the change!

Example is better than precept, so there are several manifestos by now. Because the business side of organizations did not agree with the IT focus of the first manifesto, a group of agile marketers in San Francisco published their own manifesto in 2012.

Agile marketing values

1. We value validated learning *more than* opinions and conventions.
2. We value collaboration based on customer focus *more than* silos and hierarchy.
3. We value adaptive and iterative campaigns *more than* Big Bang campaigns.
4. We value the process of customer discovery *more than* static predictions.
5. We value flexible planning *more than* rigid planning.
6. We value responding to change *more than* following a plan.
7. We appreciate many small experiments *more than* a few large estimates.

Compared with agile development values, agile marketing values are slightly more defined. It seems that they do not value, and even disapprove of, the second part of the sentence.

It is a shame that they have spent less time on the agile marketing principles. They make an initial move that is very similar to the agile development principles. Two principles are distinctly different:

1. Learning, through the build-measure-learn feedback loop, is the main measure of progress.
2. Do not be afraid to fail; learn from your failings and don't fail in the same way twice.

With an agile mindset, you will not fight initiatives for other manifestos, but rather applaud them. By thinking carefully about what your manifesto would state, painful issues are turned into valuable beliefs. Existing agile manifestos are an excellent source of inspiration in this process.

If you have a thorough understanding of the values and principles and are also convinced of the power and necessity of working according to a different belief, agile working methods will undoubtedly help you to be very valuable.

Agile working

Agile working is based on three pillars:

1. Inspect: investigate where you currently are, based on empirical data. Historical data says nothing about the future, and predictive data only yields more assumptions. Empirical data is about facts that can be observed in the here and now. To do this, develop the smallest product or product feature possible. Make sure it gets to the customer, and collect your empirical data to determine factually to what extent the customer or user experiences it as valuable. Learn based on facts.

2. Adapt: validate your assumption based on the empirically established movement (the customer is surprised, happy, confused, disappointed, etc.), and determine how it can be done (even) better. Deliver this adjustment (improved product) to the customer or user as soon as possible. Next, re-examine and determine the next instructive adjustment, etcetera. It is a continuous cycle of Inspect and Adapt.

3. Visibility: in order to be able to continuously Inspect and Adapt, all information must be completely transparent and easily accessible to all who are involved. Agile teams have an open mindset and good habits of sharing everything directly, whether asked or not, but always in an accessible way. Because a picture says more than a thousand words, agile teams prefer to visualize rather than describe in text. According to Professor Daniel Kahneman, our brains roughly have two systems: one system understands what a picture represents in a fraction of a second and the other system activates the dormant part of our brain to read text. Our brain only activates the dormant part when necessary. Because we often do not experience the necessi-

ty, much information is lost and the entire world works based solely on a part of the written information. So, forget about email, but choose to walk over to someone to draw something on a whiteboard together. Don't explain what you did in a review, but show how a user works with it. And if you provide a service, use a video or other visualization to show what the effect of the latest value addition is. If everyone has the relevant information available continuously, Inspect and Adapt will come very quickly.

Agile frameworks

Agile is part of the Lean objective to deliver the highest value with the least waste and the highest respect for people. Within the Lean objective, Agile covers the vast part that cannot be predicted. A variety of useful frameworks and methods have been developed under the agile umbrella, such as: UX, Design Thinking, Lean Start-Up, Running Lean, Growth Hacking, KanBan, and Scrum. Scrum is most commonly used by agile teams; it is the core around which the rest is configured in many agile environments. It does not prescribe anything substantial about what you should do, but helps agile teams to find an iterative rhythm within which they can work together. The Scrum rules describe how Scrum teams deal with:

- One goal: Done Product Increment
- Two lists: Product Backlog and Sprint Backlog
- Three roles: Product Owner, Scrum Master, and Development Team (together: Scrum Team)
- Five time-boxed events: Sprint, Sprint Planning, Daily Scrum, Sprint Review, and Sprint Retrospective
- Product Backlog Refinement, which is neither team-bound nor time-bound, because it takes place as needed with varying and incidentally selected participants, based on the desired expertise.

Anyone can download the Scrum Guide on the internet for free, in several languages. You can find these on the site of scrum.org.

Agile team values

In addition to frameworks, agile values also help to support agile teams in their journey to successful agile collaboration. Scrum is about the following values:

1. We have the courage to do things differently.
2. We are completely open with each other.
3. We are respectful.
4. We are focused.
5. We are committed.

It is up to the team to make this tangible in a Team Alliance. What words do they give to this? Regardless of what they come up with, the answer is right. It is their words, it is their team, and it is their partnership. It is all about making their values explicit and discussing them together in an equal dialogue. It is up to the agile coach to ensure that this happens, and to facilitate this process during team sessions. Whenever the team wants to improve their agile collaboration, they take another look at their self-made Team Alliance and enter into a dialogue about what is going well and what can be improved.

Psychological safety

For all of this to work, psychological safety is an essential foundation; otherwise the work lacks visibility, openness between the team members, respect, focus, and in the end inevitably the courage to do things differently. The agile coach examines what happens in a team based on the following five pillars of psychological safety:

1. Do we know each other? It may be obvious, but still. People feel less safe with a stranger than with someone they know. Even if the person you know is not as nice as you initially thought, you know their 'instruction manual', as it were. This results in confidence during interactions. Social gatherings help in getting to know each other as a person, so use this tool regularly.

2. Do we understand each other? Knowing each other better can also be threatening. Certain interactions between one or more teammates may cause a team member to feel constrained in their openness. When this happens, a 'storming' phase is required. In this phase, there may be some fireworks for a while, but it will help people understand each other better. This works both ways, incidentally. It usually starts with "I notice that when you... it makes me feel..." This is how you really get to know each other and create good standards of contact in the team. As an agile coach, make sure that team members do not get stuck in pleasantries and beating around the bush. They should have the courage to put their cards on the table. Continue to ask non-judgmental questions until the team has experienced the benefits of expressing their mutual irritations.

3. Does everyone belong? In a multidisciplinary team, everyone is preferably very different. This has major advantages, because it means you have something to offer each other. Unfortunately, people also have a tendency to disapprove of or exclude others who deviate from their own standards, values, or characteristics. When this happens, you lose out; it's better to open up to people who are different. Discover and make use of their potential for enrichment!

4. Is everyone involved? And are we involving everyone? Or do we subconsciously continue to involve the same people a little more than others? Is it mainly the extroverts who do the talking, or do the introverted team members have an equal say? Make an effort to involve a person who is usually less involved just as much as the others. That is often when undiscovered gold comes to the surface! I often use the sociocratic 'poker' method to achieve this, which I will discuss in more detail in this book. Teams that scrum often already know the poker method from playing poker points during sprint planning. However, you can use poker in a variety of ways in the development process of an agile team.

5. Do team members judge one another? Fortunately, people have different opinions. This applies all the more to highly educated agile professionals. But watch out for team members judging each other. Agile team members value other insights as equal to their own. They

do not contest other people's insights. Everyone must be able to trust that they can express themselves freely, which will only work if you do not judge each other. Trust arrives on foot, but leaves on horseback.

These five pillars apply to team members among themselves, but also between team members and people outside the team. And, needless to say, also in the relationship between the agile coach and the team. It is not about you as a coach, it is about the organization, the teams, and the team members. You are in it for them, not for yourself. The process is your domain, but the content is not.

Once the values, principles, frameworks, and pillars described in this chapter are familiar territory to you, and you have experienced their essence in practice, you are ready for the next step: agile coaching.

WHAT IS AN AGILE COACH?

Agile coaching in Dick-and-Jane language

When I was involved in the agile transition of ING Bank in 2014, I came across a good story about agile in Dick-and-Jane language. I asked around but no one was able to tell me who wrote it, so I cannot credit the author. I have adapted and expanded the story here and there, so that in my opinion it touches the heart of the matter even better.

One day, Dick goes to see Jane. Dick has his heart set on a really cool playground. With all sorts of things in it. Jane can build one for him, but first of all she wants to know what needs to be included in that playground. "A swimming pool, and a slide, and a sandbox, and a lot more," says Dick. Jane writes it all down in a neat little plan. Dick skims through the plan and tells Jane that she can get started, but that he wants to see everything in detail first. Jane gets to work on a chalk drawing on the sidewalk and shows Dick her work at the end of the week.

Dick is impressed. But he wants more details. "How tall will the slide be? How hot is the water in the pool? And what color will the sand in the sandbox be?" Dick asks. Jane has no idea, so she makes up all kinds of details. "Twenty yards high. And really hot. And the sand is red." Dick agrees and hands over his piggybank to Jane. "I'll be back in two weeks," he says, and off he trots. Jane gets to work. She has asked some friends from the neighborhood to come and help. "But you can't build a slide that high for that kind of money. And how hot is hot? And red sand makes your clothes very dirty," they say. "We will never be able to build it like this!" Jane is distraught. She promised Dick all these things and if she goes back he might get angry. So, she decides to get on with it as best she can. She promises her friends lots of ice cream. She takes the extra money for the slide from her own piggy bank. The water will be nice and warm, and for the red sandpit, she plans to give Dick's mother some extra detergent.

When Dick returns after two weeks, he cannot believe his eyes. It's all there, but there's not much he can do with it. There's no way he's brave enough to go on the twenty-yard high slide. The pool is too hot. And he can just picture how angry his mom will be when she sees the red stains on his pants. Dick is angry. And he wants Jane to redo the playground. Her friends don't want to help anymore because it is not even their playground and they have to be home in time for dinner. Jane starts to cry and runs to her mother.

Too bad that Dick and Jane didn't really play together. Dick and Jane could have figured out together what it should be like. But they could also have involved all their friends. Because Timmy would have had a great idea for the slide. A water slide. And Dick could have felt the water on the spot and said he wanted it cooler. And Dick's mom could have said no to the red sand and given them some nice white sand. White sand would have looked better with the water slide, turning it all into a delightful little paradise. While building the playground, they would also have found out that Dick actually cannot swim. So, they could have replaced the water with balls. Which would have been less expensive, so that they would have saved money for a seesaw. Together with their friends, Dick and Jane could have created the most beautiful playground in all the neighborhood. With a real swing, even. Because the tree they stumbled across during the building had a beautiful branch, and Jane still had a piece of rope and an old car tire.

An agile coach oversees this system and ensures that you all play together to create the best possible playground. By working together and talking to each other in a different way, you will arrive at different solutions.

New ideas will emerge that no one had thought of before. Like a swing and a ball pool. Dick would have had the playground he actually wanted, but which he could not have envisioned beforehand. And Jane could have left her piggy bank intact. And the friends from the neighborhood could have had so much fun creating the playground. They would have learned a lot from each other and they also would have solved all the issues together. Jane could have given her friends the opportunity to come up with their own solutions as long as she didn't have to smash her piggy bank. And the friends could have managed to convince Dick, and come up with even better solutions. Creating the playground would have been real teamwork, and everyone would have been happy. The agile coach did nothing about the content, but let it come about with Dick, Jane and her friends. After all, they have a lot more wisdom together than each one for themselves.

The agile coach as a system developer

As an agile coach, you help develop an organization in which people continuously learn based on empiricism, and with these learnings, exceed user expectations with new values. The agile coach helps teams and individuals discover how they can continuously deliver the highest value with the lowest risk of wasting resources. You are the purveyor of knowledge about agile organizing, thinking and doing – but you are rarely the only source. As an agile coach, you work on Willing, Knowing and Ability to achieve this.

Yes, you read that right. As an agile coach you do not do it yourself; you do not lead; you do not impose any rules, and you are not the driving force. Instead, you create awareness and get people moving. You develop an environment, indirectly, in which the good things happen while the teams are on their way to the intended goal. As an agile coach, you are an important source of inspiration, but the people around you do it themselves. They are the owner of 'what' and 'how' they can best discover, learn, develop and deliver.

As an agile coach, you connect to where the organization, the team, or individual are in their development, in other words, not where you stand. You then start developing step by step; which ensures you will move faster than you would if you were already waiting at the terminus and wondering what is keeping everyone. Make sure you are not more than one step ahead, so that self-improvement is a challenging but achievable step for the organization, the team, or the individual. People keep ownership of their development and move at their own pace. You adapt to this pace and let them take a new step every time they are (almost) ready to so.

As an agile coach, you understand very well why people want to work in an agile way in an agile organized environment. And why more and more people – but not everyone – genuinely become happier in an agile environment.

Agile coaches and scrum masters have similar goals and methods, but a different scope. The scrum master is part of a scrum team and is present on the work floor every day. He knows the team inside and out, and knows exactly what is happening. He makes sure that work is performed according to the rules of the game, facilitates scrum events, and solves problems that the team is unable to solve by itself. These will mainly be obstacles for the team that should be resolved outside the team, such as facilities, budget problems, misunderstandings, or lack of cooperation from the management, and so on. He also supports the team in the broadest meaning of the word. For example, by assisting the product owner, or by explaining to managers and employees who work with the scrum team what scrum entails and why the team works according to scrum.

Unlike the scrum master, the agile coach is not part of the team. He has an independent role and is likely to coach multiple teams and/or the management. The primary focus of the agile coach is on adopting an agile mindset and working method in the organization as a whole.

With the above, we have largely positioned the agile coach. You may find yourself thinking: "Boy, an agile coach really is a superhero", and you would be absolutely right. As described above, the agile coach is a kind of super human. Fortunately, an agile coach does not expect himself to have all the answers, however. He also creates an environment for himself in which he can learn from empiricism, so that he continuously absorbs new knowledge on the spot and while doing so discovers how he can best coach in your organization to create an adaptive value-creating environment. An agile coach does not have all the answers in advance, but goes through the same journey of discovery as the development team with things happening while you are doing it. This only works if the agile coach is very open and not afraid to be vulnerable. This includes environments where, according to the old thinking, it is expected that the agile coach is paid because he has all the answers in advance. In principle, an agile coach only has the answer to a direction and the path that will lead to the final answer that nobody knows yet.

Coach roles

As an agile coach, you have several roles that you adopt alternately or simultaneously, depending on what the situation requires. The roles are about Wanting, Knowing and Ability:

Wanting: motivating and identifying the underlying coaching question
If people don't want something, it usually won't work. If you don't want to see something, you usually won't see it. It is difficult for people to be motivated about something they cannot see (yet). There is a reason why the saying goes: "I'll believe it when I see it!". And sometimes, people say "First you believe, and then you see it." You may have heard of Johan Cruijff, a famous Dutch soccer player who was famous for his blunt and funny statements. He once said: "You can only understand something once you've figured it out." I think he learned this not by waiting for the chicken or the egg, but by just doing it. That's the quickest way to figure out how something works. If you do that, seeing and believing happen at the same time. In other words, don't start with a long training trajectory before you start, but rather while the teams have already started doing it.

The first role for the agile coach is to investigate whether the organization, team, or individual is motivated to adopt the agile mindset and working method. Pain is the breeding ground for motivation. Why would an organization want to become agile? What problem are they trying to solve?

As an agile coach, you can make the organization aware of pain that they have, but no longer experience as such. You can do this by showing how other organizations work smarter instead of harder, and explaining why that works. As an agile coach, you can then observe how your audience reacts to this and discover where the pain is. This is also called the awareness phase, in which your audience will find an understandable answer to the big question: why agile? Many agile coaches use interesting practical examples and games to achieve this. Frequently used practical examples are Nokia and Kodak (how things can go wrong) or Tesla and Coolblue (how things can go well). To allow people to experience how agile works, coaches use games such as the scrum game, UX game, innovation games, spaghetti game, or Lego games. Just try googling 'serious games' or 'game storming' and you will get a huge range of options. The best way to develop awareness is getting the participants to experience for themselves that the agile approach is faster and produces better results.

As soon as there is sufficient motivation, you investigate the coaching issue of the organization, team or individual. Where are they now and what do they want? What is their potential? The next question is: where do we start and where are we going?

No two teams are the same, and each team stands before, on top of, or behind a mountain. Or halfway, in a cave, on a country road or on a highway. No two environments are the same, and people are unique. In other words, there is no such thing as a blueprint that works for every environment, team, or individual.

When you ask about the goal of an organization, a program, or a team, you will often be presented with a clever PowerPoint presentation with an eloquently defined vision and mission. Then you ask them how long they have had these wonderful visions and missions, and whether they deliver the desired results. Don't be surprised if there is still a significant gap between the wonderful words and the realization in practice. The agile coach tries to find a better foundation to realize a mission as an agile unit. So, instead of looking at the PowerPoint, I start by considering these points:

- Is there a safe environment in which everyone wants to and can be transparent?
- Do team members actively listen to each other or mainly to themselves?
- Is there enough solidarity within the team?
- Are team members able to focus as a team?
- How do the extrinsic and intrinsic motivations of everyone who is involved in the mission interrelate?
- What valuable results do the teams deliver?

These considerations give you, as an agile coach, a good insight into where you can best start the dialogue with this team. How strong is the foundation, and where will you start? As you go along, you will quickly know whether you started at the right point and you can adjust your approach where necessary. At this point, it is not about the development path of the organization, team, or individual. To find that path, it is less relevant where you start, but all the more important that you start as soon as possible. By doing, you will see more, so that you can quickly assess the real foundation you need to find the path more quickly.

Knowing: teacher and mentor

Without the necessary knowledge, it is difficult to be able to do something. According to the ADKAR model, people go through two phases before they acquire new knowledge, and three phases before they can take action. The acronym stands for Awareness, Desire, Knowledge, Action, and Reinforcement.

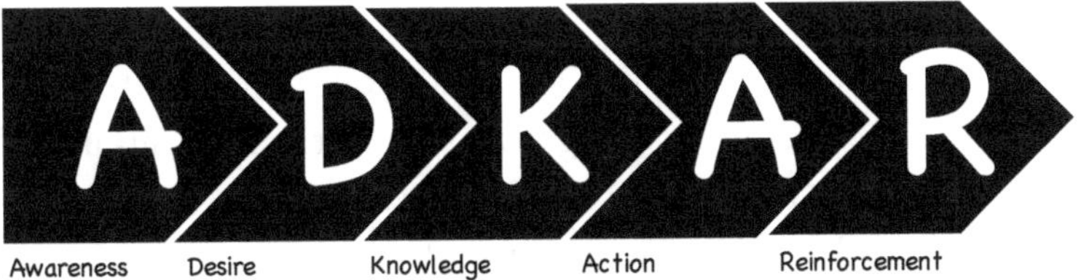

Don't be tempted to start a scrum course quickly. The ADKAR model teaches us that candidates are only ready to learn the agile approach when they are aware of its importance and are motivated to use it. Therefore, always start with awareness sessions and see if the desire for change arises. This is where the building up of knowledge starts about what agile, an agile organization, an agile team, and an agile mindset really are. But what if you notice that some candidates are not motivated? You just keep going! You cannot score 100% in the initial awareness phase. You need a critical mass of more than 50% motivated participants to start building knowledge. Accept that not everyone will be immediately motivated to change, and that the necessary awareness may take a while. Most people don't get there until they start the process. The best cure is having many open dialogues with motivated team members. As an agile coach, pay particular attention to the motivated people, this will also help the less motivated people to take the step. At first, people who are less motivated still see too many risks to really go for it. Help them by demonstrating how well the motivated people are doing. So that seeing becomes believing and daring.

Everyone learns differently, this goes for your candidates too. That is why in agile training we use a mix of lively dialogues, inventing new things, and experiencing by doing. This will suit most people.

Here is a good maxim about learning:
- What I hear, I forget.
- What I see, I remember.
- What I do, I understand *(Kong Fu Tzu, Confucius)*.

As an agile trainer, I tend to stick to:
- Pictures say more than words.
- The quickest way to learn is to try things.

Visualize as much as you can and encourage your participants to learn during games or exercises, by doing things for themselves. This includes online sessions. For online team sessions, there are some clever real-time online whiteboards available, such as Mural or Miro.

Once they have built up sufficient knowledge, the team will be able to put the agile working method into practice. Every practice is different, however, so some knowledge will still have to be invented in practice. The mentor has plenty of practical experience and is actively involved in the thinking process. He offers suggestions for a suitable approach. Please note that as a mentor, you should not make any decisions for your team; this would damage the team's ownership and autonomy. This, in turn, would lead to a decrease in the team's proactivity and intrinsic motivation.

Ability: coaching and facilitating

A coach does not bring in any knowledge and does not get involved with the content. A coach observes and notices where people are and how things are going. He is always looking for the next development step. An agile coach encourages the team members to find out together where the next step in their development is. He achieves this by facilitating the desired dialogues within the team, for example, by asking the entire team a powerful or in-depth question. He makes sure that the team discusses this among themselves in a structured manner. Once the team has adopted Pipi Longstocking's attitude: "We've never done it, so we think we can do it," this signals to the agile coach that the team is mentally in the game. At that point, the team trusts their own way of innovative thinking and their agile way of working, with which they can discover everything they need for success.

Mature agile teams constantly need inspiration, knowledge, and someone to hold up a mirror. Facilitate the team in this as needed; preferably even exclusively at the team's request. Mature agile teams that self-organize and self-manage, understand that they are in a continuous cycle in which their team competencies will level off unnoticed. That is why they appreciate an agile coach who ensures that they stay sharp as an agile team, and that they also continue to grow in their ability to learn from empiricism, together and ever faster.

Coaching Styles

Your coaching roles require multiple coaching styles. There is always a style that suits you inherently. And, of course, certain styles will not be a good match initially. Nevertheless, it is useful to become proficient in all styles, so that you can vary your style depending on the situation. In this way, your coaching will always be effective.

The listening coach

Actively listen to everything the coachee has to say, so that the coachee can create an overview of his feelings and story. This is useful if the coachee is brimming with emotions because of a situation that has arisen and cannot see the solution anymore due to the chaos.

The inquisitive coach

Ask factual questions and let the agile team tell you what the practice is. This approach allows the team to discover together what the possible improvements are, and to choose the best option themselves. This creates 'ownership' and increases their learning ability.

The reflecting coach

Ask reflection questions and hold up a mirror, to put the team members in touch with obstructing patterns in the team dynamics. As a coach, you fully rely on the agile team's wisdom.

The teaching coach

Put the agile principles, models, and experience on the table and make a 1-on-1 connection with the practical situation of the agile team.

The results-oriented coach

Set concrete objectives and a practical approach to the coaching question. Come up with exercises and propose alternatives to achieve results as quickly as possible.

The conductor coach
Ensure that all members of the team are heard in an equal way. This is useful when the drummer keeps overshadowing the guitarist, as it were. Get the team to play together in harmony.

The provocative coach
If you have established a good connection with a mature team, you can confront and encourage them with humor and a bit of a challenge. If you use this style, you need to have a good feeling for how far you can take things. Team members should not feel that you are not taking someone on the team seriously or that you are positioning yourself above the team or the individual team members. The team should experience this style as constructive, based on equality. Team members should feel able to approach you with some humor and challenge you as well.

Learn to teach every style as needed, otherwise you will develop coach allergy and lose your connection. My mother always used to say, "Anything that is preceded by *too* can't be good." Some coaches only ask questions, even at times when the coachee needs a coach to explain something. There are also coaches who continue to provoke, even when this is not constructive. The trick is to combine the styles according to the coachee's needs. If you want to give direction, you should research, teach, and work together on results in a goal-oriented way. By actively listening, reflecting, and challenging, you give the team the space to discover and learn for themselves.

Be careful not to become the scrum police, the know-it-all, the spy, or the secretary. Adopting these styles will almost certainly herald the end of your role. If it happens to you, the team has undoubtedly developed an allergy to you and it is better to stop. Learn your lesson, and start over elsewhere.

The writing style of this book is in line with the coaching styles it describes: either consciously guiding, or giving the reader space. Sometimes I will show understanding for organizations, teams, and coaches that are not yet agile; at other times I may consciously provoke in order to stimulate. Because I want to convey a lot of knowledge with this book, I will often use the teaching style. At the same time, I also want to raise questions that make readers think.

Can you already recognize the coaching styles in the writing style of this book? And can you feel the effect the different styles have on you? This is excellent input for your own introspection.

Can I become an agile coach?

The path to becoming an agile coach is different for everyone. Most really good agile coaches I know have gone through five phases in their development:
- Coaching yourself (or being coached)
- Coaching individuals
- Coaching agile teams
- Developing into an expert
- Coaching the agile organization

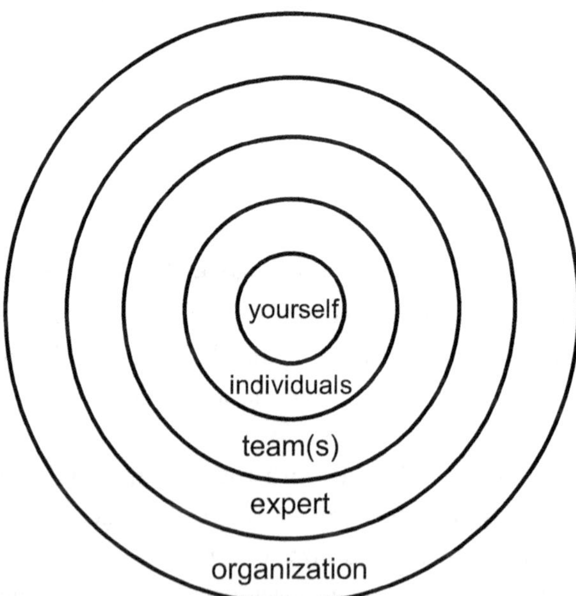

PHASE 1: COACHING YOURSELF
(OR BEING COACHED)

There are no two ways about it: a good agile coach has a wealth of practical experience and a fair amount of human knowledge. He generally has an impressive track record in developing agile organizations, agile teams, and successful people with an agile mindset. Unlike a 'regular' coach, the agile coach also fulfills the roles of teacher and mentor. In fact, the agile coach is really a facilitating TeacherMentorCoach, a coach from whom you can learn a lot based on his knowledge and experience. The agile coach is like a walking oracle through the latter. Where necessary, he can use all his agile knowledge and wisdom at any time in a value-free manner, i.e. without judging.

As an agile coach, you want the knowledge and wisdom in the agile organization to come from active practical learning. As a result, the people in the organization take ownership of the agile way of working. You will regularly face a choice between doing *something*, doing *nothing*, or *not doing something*. Whenever the wisdom in the group arises because they learn by doing, you should consciously not use your knowledge and wisdom. When this happens, you consciously refrain from responding to what you are being called upon to do, such as answering, guiding, or filling in answers. In coaching terms, this is also called not making assumptions for other people. It takes a little more time, but the learning effect is many times better than when you put words in someone's mouth.

This is why your development into a really good agile coach starts with self-awareness and self-management. Your most important tool is you, and you have to master that tool properly before you start using it. If you don't know what your triggers are, if you don't know how you got to where you are now and which of your personalities you have cast out, there is no room in your head for other people. Once you know yourself thoroughly in your capacity as a coach, you can continue on your path to coaching individuals, teams, a program or a (part of an) organization.

Introspection

How often do you question yourself? Do you find it easy to change yourself, or do you usually cling to your existing beliefs? It's a tough question, isn't it? But if you do not question yourself and are not willing to adjust your beliefs regularly, you will not be able to do so for others in your capacity as an agile coach. You have to start by examining your own shortcomings. Discover where you can feel resistance to change yourself, or are automatically inclined to sincerely think that 'the other' must change. Take the upbringing of your children, for your example. You want them to have the perfect childhood. Your ideas about the perfect childhood come directly from your own childhood memories, which are the sum of what you experienced as valuable plus what you missed out on in your teens. Actually, you want to recreate your childhood in an improved form through your children. But your children experience things very differently and, what's more, behave completely differently as well. So, what are you going to do? Are you going to try your best to convince your children of your ideal image of happy teens? Or will you allow yourself to be guided by what makes them happy now?

It may sound simple and logical, but breaking your individual old patterns is the biggest hurdle to take if you want to become a good agile coach. Once you get used to it, however, breaking old patterns and renewing becomes your new pattern, and you will be ready for the next step.

Getting to know yourself better in the first place is a huge help; this is also part of insight into human nature. You probably behave differently at work than you do at home, even if you do not experience it that way. You address your partner in a different manner than your customers, director, or shareholders. And during a sports match or at a party, you will probably behave differently again. People tend to adapt their visible personality to the circumstances. An unexpected event can suddenly turn a carefree wastrel into a serious crisis manager who makes one rational decision after another.

A person's perceptible character is determined by intuition, IQ, and EQ. Your emotional intelligence (EQ) is made up of personal and social competences. The following model can help you to take the first step to awareness of your emotional intelligence:

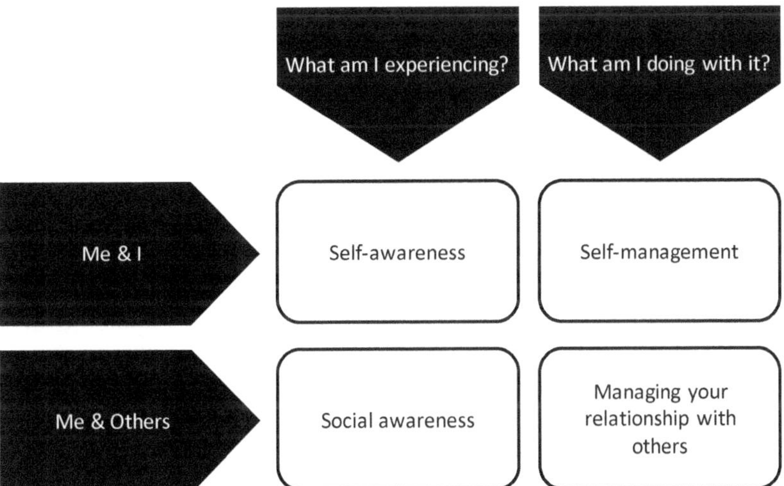

Self-awareness: are you aware of how your personal emotions affect you? And how they affect your relationships with the people around you? Do you know your red buttons, that make you feel stressed or that instantly make you climb the barricades as if stung into action? And what about your green buttons, that make you as soft as butter, so that people can manipulate you?

Self-management: how do you deal with your emotions, and is this how you want to deal with them?

Social awareness: does your response have the desired effect in specific situations? And do you recognize the emotions that you evoke in others? Are you able to discover what is happening on an emotional level with the other person? Can you understand other people's moods, behaviors, and motives?

Managing your relationship with others: As an agile coach, how do you consciously deal with the people around you in a way that improves the relationship? When agile coaches are self-aware and experiment in practice with how to consciously manage their relationships with others, this will become second nature after a while. When this happens, it becomes easier to control your own emotionally driven behavior. In order to help others with self-awareness and self-management, you will first have to learn to do this within yourself.

Once you have clarified for yourself what makes you tick and what this does to you and your environment, you can take things a step further and dive into your different personalities.

I am a big fan of the booklet 'Ik (k)en mijn ikken' (Me and my selves) by Karin Brugman, Judith Budde, and Berry Collewijn. The booklet 'Coaching with the Voice Dialogue' by Judith Budde and Karin Brugman also fits in seamlessly with this, and beautifully describes how you can apply this as a coach.

They describe in a very accessible way how your different personalities communicate with one another in your head, and how you can enter into a dialogue with them in order to make conscious and balanced choices. In the book, the authors use a jar full of selves as a metaphor. Common personalities come to life in their examples, such as the pusher, the pleaser, the politician, the dreamer, the diplomat, the inner critic, the rational thinker, the inner child, and the clown. Your well-developed primary selves often sit behind the wheel or join the conversation in the front of the bus. They push contradictory selves to the backseat, so that they never have the opportunity to develop. These selves have been rejected or expropriated, and form aspects of your personality that you are no longer aware you possess. As a result, you have a one-sided personality and unconsciously make choices based on one-sided emotions.

If you listen equally to all your selves while still making the decision yourself, your ego is in a state of consciousness. This gives your less developed selves the opportunity to develop, resulting in a nice piece of self-management, leading to a balanced personality that easily adapts when the situation demands it.

I regularly practice all the selves that get in the way or are overlooked with future agile coaches. I would recommend this practice to any coach. You literally sit on the chair of one of your selves, and start a conversation with yourself from that sub-personality. In this way, you will get to know the role and emotions of your different sub-personalities. You will also learn that while all your selves are okay, you are the one in the driver's seat making the choices, not your primary self. In other words, there is no need to change yourself as an agile coach; do stay true to yourself. Handling yourself differently is all it takes.

PHASE 2: COACHING INDIVIDUALS

After your self-awareness and self-management phase, you will help individuals in your environment to address their awareness and self-management. Coaching others is fundamentally different: now it is about other people's beliefs. You are not in control of these beliefs; the other person has complete self-determination. Your consciousness now takes on another dimension: now it is about being conscious of another person's consciousness. And on top of that, it's about how other people's beliefs affect your beliefs. See if you can, for example, set a product owner in motion using awareness and inspiration. Can you assist a product owner with his introspection? Is he aware of his own emotions, and how does he handle them? Teach the person to recognize his selves, and encourage him to engage in conversation with his selves. Once you succeed at effectively letting others take control of their own emotions, you can turn your focus to teams, programs, and ultimately an entire organization. With teams, you will need to address team dynamics, which are multiple mental models that interact with each other. At the program and organizational levels, it becomes even more complex. Here, things are no longer limited to the walls of the organization because teams, programs or organizations include those people who work together toward the same goal, regardless of whether they are employed by the same organization.

Letting go

What do you do when you see that something is not going as it should with your child? Like when your child sinks to the bottom while learning to swim at the deep end? Exactly: you intervene and take control for a short time. After a while, you hand back control because you want to give your child the space it needs to learn. We all recognize this pattern, even if we don't have children. This automatic pattern needs to be subdued when you start working with agile teams. An agile coach never takes over the reins from a team or a team member. If the team sinks to the bottom, compliment the team for being brave enough to jump in at the deep end. After all, this is where they can grow. The fact that they are sinking is nobody's fault. It's not the team's fault, nor is it the fault of the agile coach, the management, or the organization. Never try to point the finger when something goes wrong. Finding the culprit will not solve any problems. Some organizations are so busy looking for culprits that they run out of time and energy to solve the problem. When this happens, a competitor often makes off with the solution. When it comes to sensitive issues, would it not be better to simply ask ourselves: "So how should we approach it?" and leave it at that?

If you manage to create an environment that appreciates and rewards the courage to think out loud about what is possible in sensitive issues, that's when you enter the agile mindset. Leave hanging on to old patterns and looking for culprits to the rest. Let it go, and create room for valuable insights.

You can learn a lot by trying, so you can grow quickly. Welcome new insights and put them to the test. An agile team won't drown, and it's not the end of the world if something doesn't have the intended effect. Let it go, do not interfere with the content of their work, and encourage experimental behavior. Do not set new rules (such as: "From now on you can only swim in the deep end after permission"), as this only limits the team and its growth. I usually start by giving a compliment and then suggest we investigate together what could be done more effectively next time.

Analyze the process together out loud, with the team at the helm. Ask questions such as "What happened when you all took the plunge at once?". Get them to figure out the solution for themselves, and let that be their next experiment. Once they get used to this approach, you probably won't even need to ask the questions anymore. You will just have to give the compliment. At the same time, this is the moment when you may become insecure, and wonder whether you are valuable and working hard enough. After all, those around you only observe you complimenting a team whose actions do not yet have the intended effect, and doing nothing else. The team is solving things for themselves, so what are they actually paying their agile coach for? Let go of this misleading thought as well. Once you reach the stage where teams come up with the solution themselves after your compliment, you become extremely valuable as an agile coach. From that moment on, you will never be short of work, because there is plenty of demand for real agile coaches who are capable of doing just that. The value of an agile coach is not in the sweat on his body, but in his ability to introspect, get others moving, and let things go. 'Emergence' is the word that best describes this process. The agile coach takes the things that make something arise, move, and grow in the other person, and chooses whether or not to use them, and to what extent.

Shu-Ha-Ri

You may have heard of Shu-Ha-Ri: the three phases in the development of an oriental agility sport, which is also used in the adoption of agile thinking and acting.

You start with Shu: doing what the master tells you, so you can experience what it is. During this phase, you learn to recognize and understand the essence of the rules and methodologies in agile. You would not be able to do these things right without the master, so you follow the master. Once you have learned the essence based on experience, you move on to Ha. From that moment on, you start doing things the way you see them, based on what you have learned. You start to train yourself without letting go of the essence. The same applies to a retrospective session: the team continuously improves itself in a fixed rhythm. Over the years, teams have discovered many ways to conduct retrospective sessions. You may have your own new ideas to help the team improve itself. In the Ha phase, you are given the space to experiment. In this way, your understanding of the essence of agile thinking and doing improves, and agile will increasingly become a part of you. Once you have trained yourself, you are ready to serve your environment with all your knowledge and wisdom. This is when you enter the Ri phase, and you become the master. Ri represents the phase in which the goal is that your students become even better than yourself. In Shu, the student was allowed to copy everything from the master, after which he had room to experiment and enrich the agile wisdom with new best practices. He shared this sum in his Ri phase with motivated people in the Shu phase. As a result, the next apprentice has the benefit of starting with an evolved and richer Shu. They are then given the space in Ha to enrich it again, and so on. This is how agile thinking grows over time.

The only goal in Ri for a good agile coach is that his student becomes better than himself. This can be tricky if you are competitive and reluctant to be overtaken. If this is the case, the role of agile coach is probably not for you. Rest assured, there are plenty of other roles in the world that will suit you just fine. You can find many roles in sports, sales, and marketing, for example, in which you can make good use of your 'win-lose' pattern. This specific pattern in your brain says that you can only win if the other person loses. We developed that pattern in our brains as children, by playing games. In an agile environment, this is a toxic pattern that undermines the entire idea of an agile mindset. A boxing coach who teaches you how to box, on the other hand, works from a completely different mental framework than an agile coach. Agile coaches always think holistically. Shu-Ha-Ri is also a holistic growth model, without losers. Shu is part of Ha, Ha of Ri, and Ri, in turn, is the base for the next Shu. Everyone grows and everyone wins.

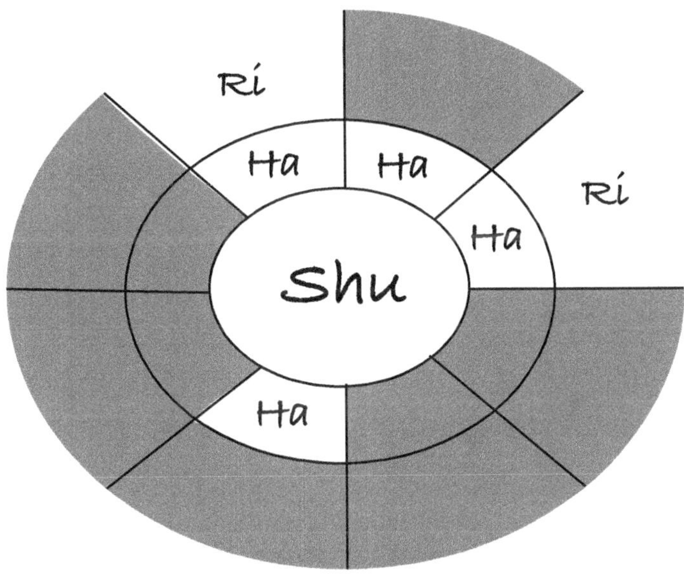

If you have the knowledge, are good at introspection and able let go, and get a kick out of seeing others around you getting better than yourself, you have what it takes to become an agile coach! Start your journey and work on as many topics as you can toward the Ri status. The journey is endless, you will always keep learning. There is no end goal; your goal is for others to become better than you. This will make you a better coach, and so on.

When can I start?

You have already started; you are reading this book. But reading a book alone won't make you an agile coach. You become an agile coach by doing, and continuously improving yourself. Build in sufficient moments of reflection with yourself, experienced mentors, and coaches. Just take a look at Edgar Dale's learning pyramid from 1946, which is still relevant today!

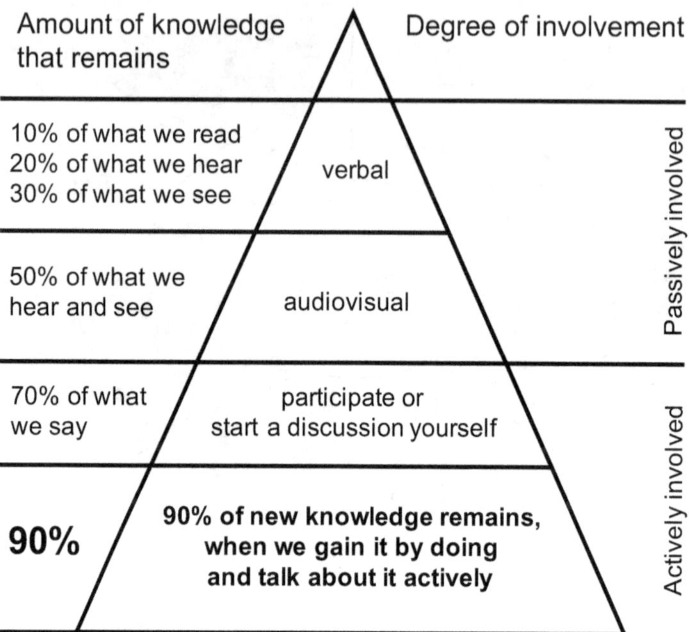

Edgar Dale was a passionate advocate of active learning by doing. It helps you to learn faster and better, and what you learn will stay with you for longer. My advice: learn actively by doing things that an agile coach does, without calling yourself an agile coach. Doing this will teach you much more than looking at what an agile coach does or reading a book about it. If this is part of the 10% you will remember from this book, this will definitely help you on your way.

Ask those around you anything you want to know, as if you were ignorant. Make use of rich communication in the transfer of knowledge, such as discussing things together while drawing out all your thoughts on a whiteboard. Do this to learn, and argue to understand rather than to be right. Agile teams similarly leverage rich communication to facilitate learning. Add this model to the learning pyramid, and you will soon have an effective method for your personal development, and for the people around you, whom you can in turn help with their development. They will also develop in this active way, faster than from a book or a lecture.

You don't have to be an agile coach to act like one. Starting today, anyone can start collaborating like an agile coach would. Simply in the position or role that you currently hold, without having the role or title of agile coach. Similarly, the people around you do not need to see you as an agile coach. There is no obstacle to simply building up knowledge in your daily practice about the possibilities of developing an agile mindset and an agile way of working together. Next, start a dialogue about this with your colleagues, teammates, or the management within the organization. Observe what happens, and try things out. The worst thing that can happen is that those around you notice you are growing faster than the rest. It is also a sign of strength if you immediately enter into an open dialogue with people around you when mistakes are made. See it as a highly effective way of learning quickly, particularly from people who immediately turn their focus to the issue of guilt. You will learn to recognize the patterns that hinder the organization, teams, and individuals in their growth. And at the same time, you will increase people's confidence to try out new things and to grow!

Once you feel that you have built up a solid foundation, try facilitating a group session. You could try this with your own team, or maybe with another team. Try facilitating a retrospective session and see what the team needs, for example. Pay special attention to yourself: can you let go of the content completely? And how do you feel when a different solution comes up than what you had in mind, like a solution from the team with which they start experimenting and learning? Try to experience that even if you don't think it's the best solution, it might still enrich the team with an experience of how not to go about things. This gives them another opportunity to find the best solution. It is their solution. And if their solution is different from your idea, it may also be better. After all, they are right in the middle of their practice. Your role is not to come up with their solution; your role is to facilitate the thinking process through which they discover their solution.

Once you notice that you are becoming adept at this, the time has come to see if you can fulfill the role of scrum master somewhere. You are then the scrum coach for a team and the product owner of that team, as well as for the part of the organization that affects that team. In this phase, try to achieve growth primarily by entering into more dialogues with the product owner and management in the organization. Also try to discover your obstructive patterns in this phase, and make a start with self-management.

The next step could be to gain experience in the role of product owner as well: literally standing in between all the stakeholders and the team. This also creates a working relationship with a scrum master or an agile coach, because the roles of product owner and scrum master or agile coach do not go together.

Have a safe journey and enjoy!

PHASE 3: COACHING AGILE TEAMS

Pulling on grass does not make it grow. And it is possible that the grass really is greener on the other side of the fence, even though the hours of sunshine and precipitation are comparable. Grass grows best if you look closely at its current condition, and what it needs. Apparently, this is the only way to create that envy-inducing gorgeous green carpet around your home. The same applies to agile teams: they don't just develop by calling them an agile team and starting to scrum. In this chapter I will explain what I mainly pay attention to with teams that I have helped to achieve great successes as an agile coach.

Teamwork

I never understood how Red Bull supposedly gives you wings. If you ask me, that drink is super unhealthy and the overdose of sugars and caffeine makes you overweight rather than light as a feather. What I do understand, is that they need Formula-1 driver Max Verstappen's performance to make their promise somewhat credible. That is why Max and Red Bull make a great team. They need each other, for their individual as well as their common purpose. Max desperately needs the sponsor money, so that he can win the competition with the best equipment. Red Bull desperately needs Max to make the target audience believe that their unhealthy drink turns you into someone who can perform big time. Although I can't imagine that it is Max's ideal to encourage young people to drink an unhealthy fattening beverage, he still has an interest in this.

The more young people buy a can of Red Bull, the more money the sponsor has to buy good equipment for Max. Conversely, it is not Red Bull's aim to spend as much money as possible on the best equipment. But if the best equipment helps Max to win, it will also make Red Bull incredibly popular. In other words: winning the race is the common goal, whereby each of the team members also has an individual interest to which they contribute cross-wise.

Working in a good team, however, can give you wings. Together, you can achieve results that would otherwise be unimaginable. A good team has synergy, in other words: $1+1=3$. It's like a relay team that runs faster than the average of all the individual records.

These are the eight characteristics of teamwork that produce synergy:
1. A clear common goal, in which every team member has an interest and an opportunity to contribute to it.
2. The required resources to reach the goal, such as time for dedication, money, equipment, systems, information, and support.
3. The mandate to realize the goal in their own way, without interference from the outside. No captains from outside the team getting involved, but ownership within the team.
4. Regular warm contacts and coordination between the team members. Even virtual teams meet physically on a regular basis, so that social interaction moments feed the team spirit.
5. Any interdependencies exist within the team, but as little as possible outside or between teams.
6. A variety of disciplines that depend on each other to achieve a common goal. In this way, the team members have plenty to offer each other and have a considerable interest in working together as a team.
7. T-shaped means that although you have depth in your discipline, you also know enough about each other's disciplines and work in progress, so that you can temporarily replace each other in the event of illness, vacation, or absence for other reasons. It also means that you can help each other when one team member has some spare time and another is extremely busy. T-shaped working also reduces the

so-called bus factor: the risk that results from failing to share information and capacities between team members, in the event a team member is 'hit by a bus'.

8. Team players have team skills, such as empathy, openness, feedback exchange, and consultation skills. They take pleasure in the social team contacts and are motivated to share everything, take on challenges together, and improvise ad hoc.

All this being said, teamwork is neither self-evident nor always desirable. Work that is predictable, and that does not involve dependence between team members, can also be done by a group of individuals. Nor should people who perform much better when they work solo be asked to work as a team. They are better off performing tasks that do not require a team setting; this is better for their happiness, the quality of their work, and the result of the organization as a system.

Phases in team maturity

An agile team has four stages of maturity: M1 to M4. The M stands for Maturity.

Characteristics of an M1 team

The team members are still trying to position themselves in the group. Does the group take you seriously when it comes to those things in which you want to be taken seriously? How does the group relate to you? We have probably all experienced in high school how far-reaching the consequences can be when you don't belong, or the group turns against you. However, not everyone is necessarily interested in being that popular person with many followers in the group. There is always an element of insecurity about a new group. The individual key question in this phase is: am I going to have an easy or hard time in this group? At this stage, the team is a group of individuals, with everyone mainly involved with themselves. And that's fine, because this is how every team starts. At the start, team members are trying to find their place within the team.

One wants to be the leader, while another may prefer someone else taking responsibility. Everyone can sense that dependencies will arise in the near future. A sort of dynamic is created.

Maturity phase M1 is common during the start-up phase of a team but not always: there are also teams that have been together for years and are still in M1.

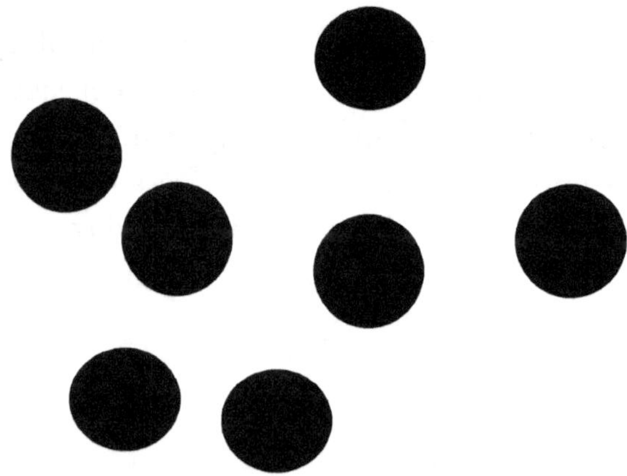

How should the agile coach deal with an M1 team?
As an agile coach, you immediately start looking at the maturity level during your introduction to the team. If the team is in M1, at the start, that is absolutely fine and to be expected. If the team is still in M1 after several months, it is high time for an intervention. As an agile coach, you will want to set up multiple introspection sessions if this happens. This gives the team the opportunity to examine themselves, and how they are doing as a team. In his role as teacher/mentor, the agile coach explains the maturity stages of an agile team and then, in his role of coach/facilitator, ensures that a healthy dialogue arises about the team's maturity. Where are they and how is that apparent? Where do they want to be and how will they get there? The outcome of the introspection session is that the team proposes one or more actions to carry out themselves, to break through old patterns in their maturity and to promote their development toward the next maturity phase. The agile coach regularly asks about this and, particularly, encourages the team members to regularly discuss this

among themselves. Not to call the team to account, but because he wants to keep the dialogue alive that helps the team to develop.

Characteristics of an M2 team

During this phase, coalitions are formed in the team. Fortunately, people in an agile team tend to have strong opinions. They also like to discuss these opinions with their teammates; this is a healthy habit that you should definitely encourage in your role of agile coach. As a result, like-minded people among the team members will start to agree with each other. However, not everyone thinks the same way; this is especially true in multidisciplinary teams that are preferably as diverse as possible. This creates several coalitions within a team. These coalitions usually consist of two or three team members who share an opinion on a particular topic that conflicts with the opinion of two or three other team members. You guessed it: this is an interesting phase in the team's development toward maturity! It may even lead to uncomfortable conflicts. Sometimes insecurity strikes and you find yourself wondering whether it is such a great team after all. Shouldn't agile teams always be happy and brimming with energy? Not to worry. Maturity phase M2 is a tricky one, but it is also very useful in shaping the character of the team. You could compare it with puberty, when it becomes difficult to understand one another's values. This phase is necessary in order to grow into the adulthood of M3, where people feel safe to express any dissent. In M2, you discover that you are more valuable as a team if you do not get stuck in a polite little tea circle.

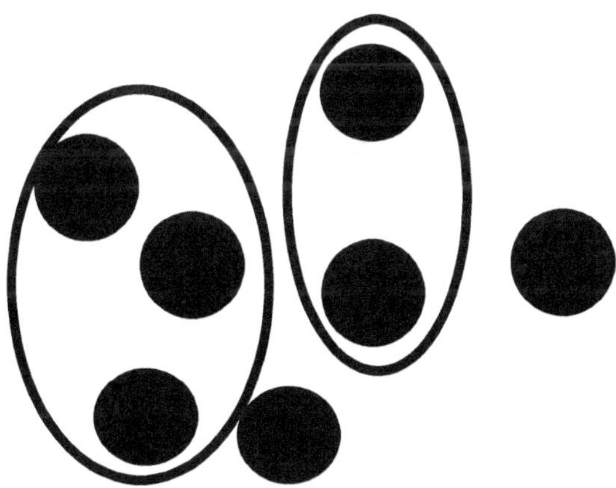

How should the agile coach deal with an M2 team?
Be careful not to fall for the many potential pitfalls in this phase. I have known agile coaches who tried to calm these kinds of conflicts with individual conversations, or started laying down the outcome of the conflict to the entire team. That's 'old school management', and a futile attempt to lead a team. It is considered a mortal sin for agile coaches, because this can never lead to maturity phase M3 – let alone M4. If this happens, the team will not develop into a self-organizing team but into a docile reactive team. And it will not deliver more than what you would expect from a traditional, hierarchically managed team. Teams like this have usually been whisked back to maturity stage M1, so this approach is hardly useful to us in an agile environment.

First of all, an agile coach must be able to oversee what is really going on. The team is developing from a group of individuals (M1) into a team (M3). So rather than fight the symptoms, it's a cause for celebration! These are useful conflicts that a coach can put to good use to teach the team how to share their opinions without reservation, beyond the polite tea circle, openly and freely. Pay attention to two points at this stage:

1. Have a conversation with the entire team about what it would mean if the team learned to cast out the ego-based thinking that the team experienced in M1. And discuss how they can grow in eco-thinking: how are we going to collaborate together fruitfully and for a long time?

2. Next, enter into a conversation with the entire team to discover the added value of thinking differently. When you think differently, you have something to offer each other, you can enrich one another! The team has grown when they agree that they don't want to talk about the person, but always about the content.

It really helps to introduce the sociocratic circle discussion in this phase, where people learn not to judge each other's opinions too quickly, but to listen to each other respectfully first. Further on in this book, I will come back to how to conduct a sociocratic circle discussion.

Characteristics of an M3 team

This is the winning team. The team members see each other's differences as particularly valuable and can discuss them together in a completely open and constructive manner. Communication and collaboration have acquired a true sociocratic character, and the agile principles characterize the collaboration style. Teams like this stand out in the organization; they are usually much more successful than other teams. And the team knows it, too. Because they deliver evidence every day, the team also thinks itself better than the rest. M3 teams do not see this as arrogant, but as a fact. This also has a flipside: the team will subconsciously feel the need to continue to be the winning team. Team members will feel that the team should not welcome new members just like that, and create a kind of balloting, as it were. They feel that only this team can handle the best challenging projects, and that it would be a sign of mismanagement if they were given to another team… You get the picture: a kind of competitive field emerges in the organization around the winning team. This can strengthen the self-confidence and success of this team. For the rest of the organization, however, this is counterproductive.

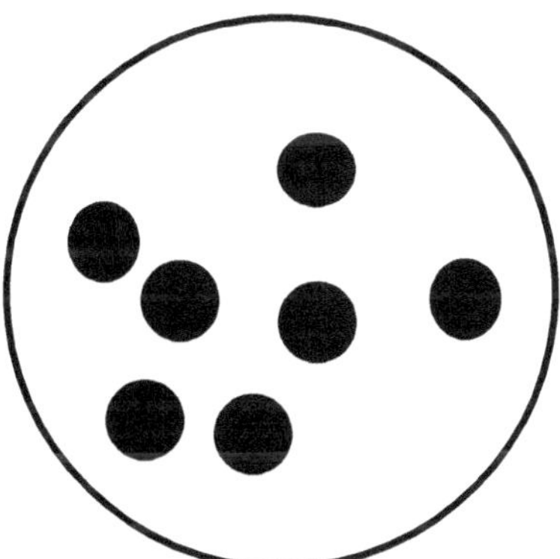

How should the agile coach deal with an M3 team?

At this stage, it is high time for a good talk with the team, to grow toward M4. Compliment the team and express your appreciation and admiration for their strength. Visualize the four stages of maturity and briefly explain them. Ask the team where they think they are. Some team members will undoubtedly rate their team as M3 or M4. Explain how everything in the world is connected in a holistic way, and relate this to the organization. Explicitly state how the ultimate success of their team also depends on the rest of the organization. At this stage, you need to make sure that the group dialogue does not resort to blaming. Ask the team what hinders them in growing even more toward M4 maturity, and what will actually contribute to improving the team as a holistic part of the organization.

Characteristics of an M4 team:
A mature M4 team assumes that the organization is a holistic unit. In other words, everything is part of something else. For example, the team is part of an innovation program, which is part of an organization. This organization, in turn, is part of a society, and so on. I realize that this is a pretty crude representation of a holistic entity, but this is about the essence of an entity in the context of growing from M3 to M4. In M4, the team acts as a part of the larger entities. Although the members form a team, they work together integrally and as equals with their environment, even if this environment performs less well than the team itself. M4 teams understand that they would be nothing if they were on a deserted island without this environment and that they would ultimately achieve poorer results. They do not keep things to themselves and share all their knowledge and experience. Their ambition is for their environment to become even better than they are themselves, in the full conviction that this will make them grow in turn. And growing together is even better than growing alone with your team!

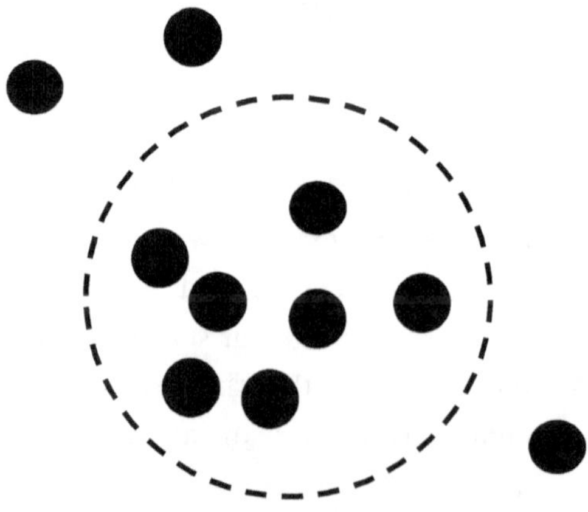

How should the agile coach deal with an M4 team?

A mature agile team needs a mature agile coach. Even the most successful team evolves in a cycle in which the flattening of maturity and relapsing into old patterns are not unusual. This cycle goes from consciously incompetent to consciously competent, unconsciously competent, unconsciously incompetent, and then full-circle to consciously incompetent. Because mature teams know that this cycle continues to repeat itself, they ask an agile coach to regularly hold up a mirror. As a coach, you confront, or let the team confront itself, by asking powerful questions or provoking paradoxical interventions that make the team think. The goal is to raise awareness in the team whenever their incompetence subconsciously creeps back in. This will allow the team to regain their inherent competence.

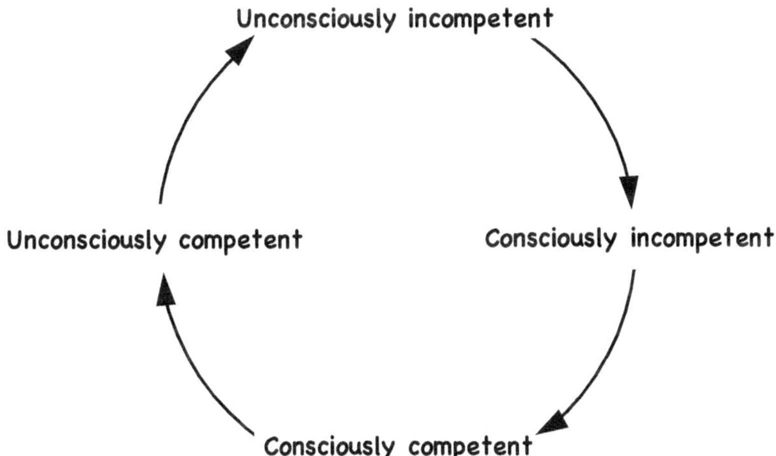

While with an M1 team you can still expect to be very proactive as an agile coach, with an M4 team you will need to be reactive. In other words: check how things are going from time to time and where you should hold up the mirror. If necessary, you can visualize the maturity stages again to facilitate a good group dialogue and take action if the team so requests. That's it!

Team formation

As an agile coach, people will regularly ask your advice when forming teams. How do you put together an agile team? What are the team and personal characteristics? How do we tackle this?

It is useful to realize that an agile unit does not start by forming a team, which is subsequently ready to decide what to do. If that were true, us agilists would just be in the business of job creation. Instead, agile units are all about value delivery. In other words, it starts with a vision of the value the agile unit wants to deliver, and for which end user. Once we have a clear view of the value we want to deliver, we can gain insight into the value carriers, better known as the products. For the products, we appoint a product owner who has sufficient affinity with the end user to be able to represent their interests. The product owner estimates what expertise he will need to develop the product, without dependencies from outside the agile unit. And so the product owner puts together an end-to-end team, i.e. a multidisciplinary team with motivated professionals who can make the entire product. Incidentally, this does not necessarily need to be the product owner's task alone; the management may want to assemble a team or the team may do so in self-organization. My preference is that the product owner is closely involved at the very least. After all, he is responsible for making sure that the value is delivered. If this requires more than nine professionals, it is best to split them into multiple teams. Nine is the maximum number whereby people still experience a connection as a team. Having more team members leads to coalitions or sub-teams within the team. For the team composition, choose the various disciplines that are most interdependent on each other in the daily development work, in order to be able to develop the entire product from start to finish. This is especially important for the critical dependencies. You will end up with multiple teams, but they still form an agile unit together. There is intensive cooperation within the teams, and between the teams on a regular basis.

The next question is who you want on the team. Is every professional suitable for working in an agile unit? Most certainly not! Some people do not enjoy the dynamics of an agile team, which makes it difficult to create the right chemistry. People who like certainty and predictability tend to slow down the development process unnecessarily. After all, this process consists of a lot of uncertainty and plenty of experimentation. This requires a growth mindset, which I often find in people I like to describe as 'rebels with a cause'. They like to color outside the lines. Not to be contrary, but to discover new things that you simply would not discover when you color inside the lines. In other words, they have cause to think differently. Lateral thinkers do this at the many promising instances when this is valuable for the value they are creating. Professionals who think differently from the general opinion also have the most to add. But how do you find this type of rebellious professional who thinks differently? The difference between potentially docile and rebellious team members is easily noticeable in an everyday conversation. But how do you distinguish between rebels with or without a cause? In my experiments, I noticed that rebels without a cause are frustrated people. They are angry and talk reproachfully about others, or about a system that is all wrong. Their cause to rebel is frustration. They are still in the early stages of developing into a useful rebel, and are not yet ready for an agile entity. My guess is that about half of these rebels grow into a useful rebel with a cause. They are the ones who are fortunate enough to have experienced that dealing with their frustration in a constructive manner makes them happier. They have discovered that they can improve the world not by looking for the culprits, but for the solution. The other half will unfortunately remain frustrated for life and put a lot of effort into proving that it's someone else's fault. So, pay close attention to how someone talks:

1. The yes-man swims with the tide and agrees with everything you say. → Not suitable.
2. The security seeker is mainly interested in how things will pan out exactly, and hates surprises. → Not suitable.
3. The rebel without a cause is trying to prove that the system is no good, and who is to blame. → Not yet suitable. However, this person has the

potential to become a suitable rebel with a cause. You can take the risk if you expect the person will be happy to be coached. The foundation is there, so estimate your own coaching qualities with regard to this person.

4. The rebel with a cause is trying to think of new ways to improve things that may be frustrating. The end justifies any means as long as no one is harmed in the process. → Suitable!

Rebels with a cause can easily be recognized by their curiosity, eagerness to learn, and the bags of positive energy they radiate. They invented the concept of giving meaning, and they are straining at the leash.

This is all well and good in theory, but in practice, according to the list we mentioned earlier, only a small group is suitable for a successful agile environment. You will probably get an influx of all types in your team. So, use the list mainly as inspiration for team members whom you want to help in managing themselves, for a fruitful agile collaboration. I have seen senior yes-men flourish, and their true nature emerge, during an agile transition. It turned out that in their spare time they were the rebels with a cause, and saw work as a place to rest after their efforts. Now they were able to reverse this pattern and absolutely flourished at work!

And then you have the perfectionists among the rebels with a cause. Perfectionists think the product is nowhere near good enough to present to customers. This makes them think the team should only validate products with real users late in the development process. Perfectionists become more effective in an agile environment once they redefine the word 'perfect'. In the agile mindset, 'perfect' means that a customer can use it as quickly as possible, so that the team can learn how to improve it. This ultimately leads to the development of a fantastic product with as little loss of time and budget as possible. In an agile environment, perfectionism is not in the product, but in the perfect development process.

Don't be afraid of outsiders. In fact, preferably look for people whose ideas are different from the average beliefs in the organization. Do make sure that they are creative go-getters, who do not sit around and wait until they get an assignment, but prefer to take the initiative themselves.

There is added value in hiring people who have teachings to offer the team or organization. Otherwise, you just end up hiring warm bodies who do what they are told and do not add any developmental work. I regularly discuss a famous statement by Steve Jobs with management and HR: "It doesn't make sense to hire smart people and then tell them what to do; we hire smart people so they can tell us what to do." Hire motivated professionals so that you can fully focus on the process right from the start to create the highest value, in the shortest time, and with the least risk.

Safe Environment

Once the team has been formed, you will first want to create a safe environment. I am not talking about health and safety certificates for the workplace here, but about a psychologically safe environment where people feel at liberty and unafraid to express themselves without reservation.

You expect the team members to work together transparently and use their full potential in creativity. You create a safe environment in the first place by removing any barriers that prevent people from expressing themselves. For example, when people do not know each other yet, they will experience a barrier to speak frankly about everything. And if they experience disadvantages from expressing their opinion openly, they will do so less often. Do not underestimate the influence of the management, the product owner, and yourself as an agile coach. If you set the right example by expressing all your thoughts and also publicly appreciating others when they do the same, you are proving to them that this is safe. Never get personal, and welcome every opinion. See dissenting voices as an enrichment rather than a threat.

In the team dynamics of agile teams, psychological safety is by far the most important foundation for success. Professionals who experience more psychological safety are less likely to leave the organization, more likely to harness the power of the different ideas of their teammates, and more than twice as effective in creating value, on average.

Amy Edmondson, an organizational behavior scientist and Harvard University professor, first introduced the concept of 'team psychological safety'. Edmondson defined it as, "a shared belief held by members of a team that the team is safe for interpersonal risk-taking." Asking a question in a team may be perceived as if you are insufficiently informed. Moving on without getting clarification and thus avoiding the risk of being perceived as ignorant may seem an easier option. I know that in many organizations this happens every day. You can sense the elephant in the room, but nobody dares to address it. In such organizations, people don't hold each other accountable for things that could be improved. And if this does happen, the person feels mentally attacked or team members go on the defensive. The team is docile and seems to have no opinion of its own. This is the seemingly harmonious team that gets stuck in the polite tea circle and does not dare to take risks.

In order to estimate the psychological safety level of a team, Edmondson formulated several statements. You could ask the team to tell you to what extent they agree or disagree with these statements. This is not so much a measurement as an invitation to an open dialogue in which the agile coach can observe what is happening – particularly in the team's dynamics. It is not about *what* people say, but mainly about *how* they say it. Observe emotions, such as who is the first to state an opinion and who seems extremely hesitant to offer an opinion, even if you ask them outright.

These are, roughly, the statements formulated by Edmondson:
1. If you make a mistake on this team, it is often used against you.
2. Members of this team are able to raise problems and difficult issues.
3. People in this team sometimes reject others because they are different.
4. It is safe to take a risk for this team.
5. It is difficult to ask other members of this team for help.

6. No one on this team would deliberately act in a way that undermines my efforts.
7. By collaborating with members of this team, my unique skills and talents are appreciated and used.

The team can work on its own team psychological safety by facilitating a good dialogue about these propositions. After the observation, you take stock for yourself and estimate what the next step should be to improve the team's psychological safety. Edmondson gives three tips to this end, which can be applied by the agile coach as well as the individuals in and around the team:

1. Consider the issues that arise from the statements as a learning point, not as an implementation problem.

Don't argue about the reason or the culprits. As an agile coach, ask the team which aspect they want to improve first; what would help them the most in becoming a healthy or healthier agile team. How do they want to go about this? Help with suggestions, if necessary: you are not just a coach who asks questions (that causes coach allergy), but also a teacher and mentor.

2. Recognize your own fallibility.

No one is infallible. People are not perfect, and making mistakes is inherent to being human. No big deal, in other words. Don't pay too much attention to the mistake that was made. Openly acknowledge that you make minor and big mistakes yourself as well, and share what you learn from them. Ask others to share their minor and big mistakes as well, and what they have learned from them.

3. Model curiosity and ask plenty of questions.

Encourage the team to have positive experiences with asking questions. For example, by having everyone ask at least one question per topic in sessions. Once asking questions comes naturally to the team, it also feels safer for all the team members to ask questions, particularly when they experience that asking questions really helps. Setting the right example doesn't hurt here. Start by asking ignorant questions about anything that is not 100% clear to you. I bet you will discover more than you thought!

Sociocracy

In an autocracy, a single person (or committee) holds the reins. In a democracy, everyone has an equal vote and the majority of the votes count. An autocracy yields quick decisions, but does not guarantee the quality of these decisions. A democracy is valuable, but having the most votes does not guarantee the quality of decisions either – especially when influenced security seekers, yes-men, and rebels without a cause get equal voting rights. We can all list several world leaders who gained power thanks to protest votes from rebels without a cause and yes-men or followers. From a rational point of view, this choice is not logical, but unfortunately this is how the masses choose relatively bad (often populist) leaders in relatively bad times. The masses hope that this bad leader will deal with the parties who, in their experience, are guilty of the bad situation. In other words, they expect the elected leader to do something they cannot do themselves. And although things usually go from bad to worse after that, it seems we don't learn from history and fall into the same trap over and over again, albeit democratically. Among the suitable rebels with a cause, a democracy might work, but a sociocracy works better. A sociocracy is not about a person, egos, votes, or a steering committee. In a sociocratic agile unit, we don't want to predict the future, but we do want to learn quickly. Agile units believe that first of all you should listen to each other's vision and arguments with the utmost respect. The idea is not to have a free-for-all meeting with endless discussions, but to set a time limit and deploy skills to share each other's views and arguments to the point. Every team member has a sincere desire to understand the different opinions, because often even the most exotic opinion contains very valuable elements. However, most people cannot yet see that value, and our brains perceive the opinion of the group as safer than anything that deviates from the group. Many people also think too much in terms of impossibilities from the past. Our brain prefers things we know over something we don't yet know. The final questions in a sociocracy are therefore always "How then?" and "Would it hurt if we tried this?". A sociocracy breaks through the barriers of our brain and promotes innovative thinking and constructive action. Decisions are never set in stone and can be changed at any time, if we have tried something and find that it can be done better. Cooperation in a sociocracy is best described as an ongoing open experiment with a focus on continuous improvement.

Storming and norming

When you form an agile team, the start is always great fun. The team is allowed to create valuable things together in a stimulating way with plenty of autonomy. It's exactly what a suitable rebel is looking for in life. It all starts with introductory sessions: fun social events where team members really get to know each other and the necessary foundation of trust for good collaboration is created. People get a taster of the open atmosphere and everyone is motivated to get on with it. There is plenty of energy in the air and the team gets off to a flying start. The team members immediately show that they can deliver a result in a short time. Everyone wants to continue like this, but this turns out to be unrealistic in practice. After the polite tea circle, personalities start to rear their heads. The team members have not read one another's user manual yet, as it were. Knowing everyone's personal standards and values is quite a step beyond socializing. Like-minded people will find each other, but they may also form a coalition against dissenting voices. Subconsciously, everyone wants the others to adopt their standards, which is easier than adjusting your own standards and values. Plus, rebels have strong beliefs, standards and values. So, this phase yields some friction and conflict. And that's a good thing. Finding out about each other's manuals is a journey of discovery. And as long as you don't disrupt this process, the team members will find these manuals. They need this manual to form a close-knit team, so it's important that they work their way through this phase properly. Many team members will come knocking on the door of their agile coach to draw you into the coalition. Don't go along with this and ask if they have thoroughly pored over the outliers' point of view. What makes different team members have different norms and values? Do they stand in the way of proper collaboration? How do you deal with that? Make the other person think. The answers are not there for the taking, so team members will have to engage in conversation to really understand each other. Sometimes they get stuck in the conflict, and it is time for the agile coach to organize a dialogue session. A group session with the core qualities of Ofman is usually the way to go.

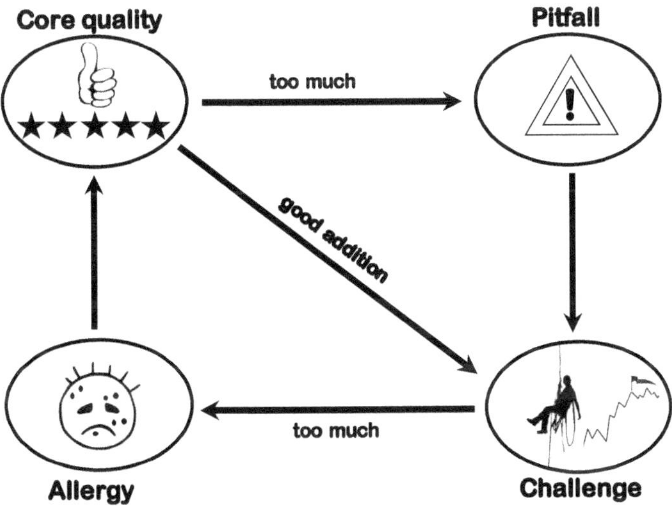

Draw the canvas per person on a large A0 format. Ask the team members to indicate for each other and themselves what qualities they perceive and when they feel these are taken too far.

In this way, team members get to know the three faces of their qualities as well as their challenges. Every team member will learn a lot about themselves through the eyes of the other team members. They also learn where everyone's allergies are. Everyone's personal challenge is a good addition to their personal core quality. The challenge is to prevent people from going too far in their core quality, but at the same time not to go too far in their challenge. For example, a person can be very modest, and therefore listen carefully to what another person says and means. His core quality is his empathy. The consequence may be that if he does this excessively and becomes less visible as a result, that people will not know what he thinks. This creates a distance that can turn his strength into a weakness. His challenge is then to position himself better and also to regularly put forward his opinions. He experiences overshooting in positioning oneself as arrogant, which is inherent in his allergy. By mutually discussing the quadrants like this within the group, they will learn to better understand each other's and their own manuals.

The outcome of the storming phase is that team standards are created that enable the team to become a high-performing team. Bruce Tuckman, the American social psychologist, described this in 1965 in his psychological model for group dynamics.

According to Tuckman, a team will never perform well as long as it has not gone through joint conflict and set standards for behavior. Unfortunately, more than half of all agile transitions end before the norming phase, because people are not prepared to go through the storming phase. I have been sent packing from a bank by a manager when I had just had a fantastic storming phase happen in a team. The manager was

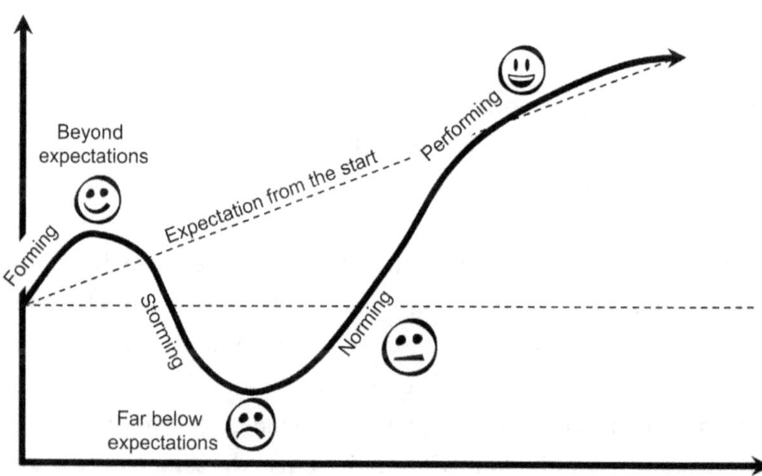

disappointed because he had hired me to nurture a happy team. And I had failed to include the manager in this thinking beforehand, so hopefully that won't happen to me again.

In a high-performing team, there is also an adjourning phase: when a team breaks up again. Keep an eye out for this phase, because for close-knit adult agile teams, the team feels like family. They know each other through and through, and trust each other blindly. Moreover, they have accomplished great results together. You cannot just tell them out of the blue which family members will be assigned to a new family tomorrow. This feels like a forced marriage, and in doing so you will extinguish the shining stars of your organization. You can build up this process by starting over from the perspective of each team member separately with a dialogue about the meaning of that other family. Next, ask them to think about it. Give it time and leave the ball in the team member's court. The team member must be encouraged to leave the nest. You will notice that it happens faster than you would expect and that the transfer is successful. Make sure you offer a positive and dignified farewell, including for those who stay behind because they will lose a family member. Fortunately, they will see that their relative has thought about this and is moving to a place where he will be happy. Team members of high-performing agile teams are not simply resources that you can move around as you like. They are talents who belong to a close-knit family.

Team spirit

Team spirit is the mental model of a team, also known as the chemistry in the team. In other words: what makes the team members form a good team together?

You can recognize a healthy agile team by:
1. their shared vision and approach;
2. continuous learning and improvement;
3. regularly delivering concrete results;

4. situational awareness;

5. the ability to grow by continuously adapting to the changing environment.

An agile coach naturally wants as many healthy agile teams as possible. But how do you know the state of the team spirit of your teams? Every team is unique!

I sometimes draw a large bottle on an A0 canvas, and ask team members to write on post-it notes what team spirit means to them. Ask them to stick what they experience in the team inside the bottle, and what they don't, but want to, experience outside of it. It is always wonderful to see how participants tell each other with conviction what team spirit means to them and how it works. What they write is literally the spirit of this particular team, which ensures that the team always thinks based on the whole and not as a group of individuals. The bottle is the metaphor the team uses to explicitly visualize when their genie is in or out of the bottle. After their personal interpretation of team spirit, the team members engage in conversation about each post-it note, and discuss what would ensure that their valuable pieces of team spirit stay inside the bottle. Or which pieces of team spirit they feel are lacking and how they can get these into their bottle.

During this session, the agile coach observes to what extent the agile principles are actually present in the mindset of the team:

1. *The team regularly delivers value*
   Does the team know what value is? Do they think in terms of distinctive value for the customer or user? And do they know the power of surprising customers and users with values that they have not yet asked for? Do they know the leverage effect of value creation for any conceivable goal?

2. *The team welcomes change, even at a late stage in the process*
   Do they like to keep adjustments at bay, or are they willing to throw away their own work as soon as it appears that achieving the intended value in a different way is a better idea?

3. *Real users validate the value to the team*
   Does the team leverage many small and affordable experiments that can be put into practice quickly, with real users, who are preferably unaware that they are part of a test? Are they doing this to learn, or to prove themselves right?

4. *The team works together with their environment*
   Do the team members work equally transparently with other teams, inside and outside of the organization? Or do they prefer to keep knowledge and skills within their team?

5. *The team stimulates the development of one another's talents*
   Does every team member like it when another team member becomes the best player?

6. *The team communicates directly and respectfully*
   Are the team members still in the polite tea circle phase, avoiding the storming phase? Or have they at least reached the norming phase, and do they know how to address each other openly?

7. *The team has a sustainable rhythm, which the team members can maintain for a long time*
   Does the team take on mountains of work, or allow others to inundate them with work? Or do they save some space to look around them and to work together?

8. *The team prioritizes the work*
   Is there good cooperation with the product owner about the relatively weighted priorities and development strategy? Is the main focus of the team on the joint (sprint) goal? Is the goal based on value or on work?

9. *The team makes autonomous decisions without egos, based on consent or facts*
   What influence does the HIPPO (Highest-Paid Person's Opinion) have on the team? Does the most dominant team member's opinion prevail? Does the team consider every opinion no more than an assumption until it has been empirically validated? If a valuable experiment cannot cause harm, does the team decide to take on the experiment (consent)?

10. *The team reflects on and improves its own working methods*
   Is the team happy to hold up a mirror regularly? And do they conclude that someone outside the team has to change something, or always someone within the team? Are any improvements actually implemented in the team?

Based on your observation, decide what might be a suitable next step for the team, and what this would require from you as a teacher, mentor, coach, or facilitator. This is about a team and as an agile coach you want to promote the team spirit, so your preference should be to let things happen during team dialogues wherever possible. Your aim is to bring out knowledge based on common sense. If desired, confirm this with practical examples, ask in-depth questions, and find out what the team needs in order to take the next step.

To engage in a dialogue with the team, I often use a modified version of how people at Google view the minds of their teams. I do this by presenting the team with one of the following statements to start a sociocratic circle discussion:

1. We are not afraid to speak up, while taking others' feelings into account.
2. We do a good job, while also delivering on time.
3. We know our goals and prioritize our work.
4. Our work gives us meaning because it impacts others.

Spotify's Squad Health Check Model is also an excellent method for entering into a dialogue with the team. The team then uses traffic light cards to express how they experience their health based on agile principles. Please note, this is not an assessment to form a judgment about a team. Agile coaches use this exclusively to facilitate a lively team dialogue. When I use this type of resource, the results of these tests go straight into the paper shredder at the end of the session. If the team gets even the slightest inkling that they are being judged through this, you will have lost a piece of the trust that is so very important for a safe and open cooperation.

Team focus

Does the team have a shared vision on the value they want to deliver, and for whom? Does every team member have a crystal-clear picture of the highest priority? And are they not juggling too many balls on the side? Multi-tasking sounds good, but doing lots of things also means paying 'switch costs' every time you change tasks. Your brain needs to park the task you have just finished, as it were, which expends time and energy. And your brain has to start up again for the task you are about to tackle, which also takes time and energy. In the past I have attended meetings where the participants were only just becoming sufficiently attuned toward the end of the meeting. Sadly, the meeting was over before they were ready and off they went, to the next meeting where the process was repeated. There was no focus, and no productivity either. They were like a dog chasing its own tail.

Check that the team has sufficient focus – as a team, that is. And make sure their switch costs aren't getting out of control. Once a team is lagging behind due to different ideas about priorities, it will go into a downward spiral and start delivering less and less. The agile coach should visualize the cumulative switch costs for the team. This will help them to conclude for themselves that their available time to deliver value is decreasing due to their lack of focus. The agile coach works with the Product Owner to ensure a shared vision on value and priorities.

Intrinsic motivation

People can be extrinsically motivated with bonuses, a good salary, and a company car. However, their effect on better performance is only temporary. You can hold on to people with these elements, to avoid them working for your competitors. This usually works just fine, but it has the same effect as an addiction. Junkies are addicted to the extrinsic reward which creates a dependency. As a result, higher rewards often lead to poorer performance. Excuse me? Does that not make sense? In his book Drive!, Daniel Pink offers a transparent account of his scientific research into this striking phenomenon. You can find the short version in a video animation on YouTube. Better performance comes from an intrinsic motivation. Pink argues that you should simply remunerate people fairly for their work, i.e. not under or overpay them. This will provide space for creating and improving their intrinsic motivation, which consists of purpose, autonomy, and mastery.

For an agile team, this means being well aware of which pain they are going to solve for whom (purpose). That they have to experience sufficient space to discover for themselves how they can best solve that pain (autonomy) and that they also want to continuously improve them-

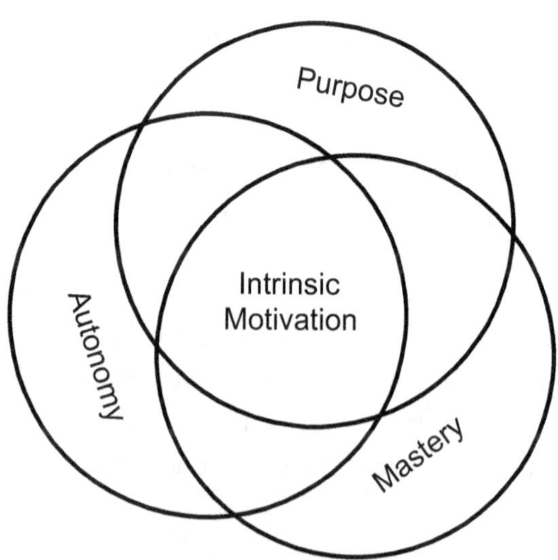

selves (high-performing in customer delight). In short, they should experience that they can grow under their own steam, and are valuable. The agile coach observes the teams and decides whether the team consists of junkies, or professionals with an intrinsic motivation. Doing so immediately tells you which intervention to use. Organize a session for participants to play around with the things in their work that make them happy and the things they hate. I often frame it as 'the job you love' and 'the job you hate'.

Cluster the results in the three circles and voilà, your user manual is ready. Tell the team about Drive! by Daniel Pink, and ask them what needs to be done. If the team indicates that something should happen in a different way from what you had in mind, the team is right. You could ask a few ignorant questions about it if you must, but the team owns its own development.

Team performance

Team performance is a result of all the previous building blocks. Think of it as a sum: a well-formed team + knowledge + skills + a safe environment + sociocracy + well-completed storming and norming + team spirit + team focus + intrinsic motivation = the best team performance! You could also read this the other way around. If team performance is lagging, it often lacks intrinsic motivation, team focus, team spirit, team norms, sociocratic decisions, a safe environment, or a well-formed team. Estimate where the team members currently are with respect to all these items, and challenge them to take their first step forward.

Team mandate

A self-organizing team has autonomy and a mandate to make its own decisions to a certain extent. This is easier said than done, however. Simply telling a team that they can decide everything for themselves from now on is not enough, but you shouldn't try to stop your children from growing either. It's like a transitional model.

Suppose your decision-making power is greater than your skills to fulfill that power. What do you do in that case? When this happens, most people will be afraid that someone will discover that they cannot do this at all, so they will behave as inconspicuously as possible in the organization. They will certainly want to avoid entering into heated discussions. They will swim with the tide of others' opinions because when things do go wrong, it will not be as a result of their inability and they will not be blamed. Does this remind you of someone you know?

Suppose you have more skills than actual powers to put your skills to good use. Whenever you try to contribute your knowledge and skills, you are brought to heel and someone will make it clear to you that this is not for you to decide. What do you do in that case? You will probably stop putting that energy into your organization, and you will take up a challenging hobby where your qualities are recognized and produce value. Or you take a job elsewhere, taking all your value with you. These examples do not contribute to the development of people or teams. Too much or not enough mandate will not contribute to an agile organization – on the contrary.

You want the mandate to match what the team is able to handle. Moreover, you want to challenge the team so that they develop more and more skills and can handle more mandates. Until, with a full mandate, they can be not only self-organizing, but also successfully self-managing. And, by definition, deliver more value than a team that needs managing.

Agile teams get into a flow when the mandate suits the skills. It makes teams open up and engage in constructive discussions. They have a sense of ownership and take responsibility. When they get down to work, their energy is released and they give it to the organization. They rest in their spare time and blossom at work.

Teams grow when they are challenged at the top of the flow channel. The trick is, therefore, to establish where the team stands, and to give them a mandate they can handle if they try their best. You then stretch the mandate as the team grows, to an ever more challenging level. The team can now feel itself growing, which is incredibly stimulating and motivating. As a result, the stretch can be applied more and more widely.

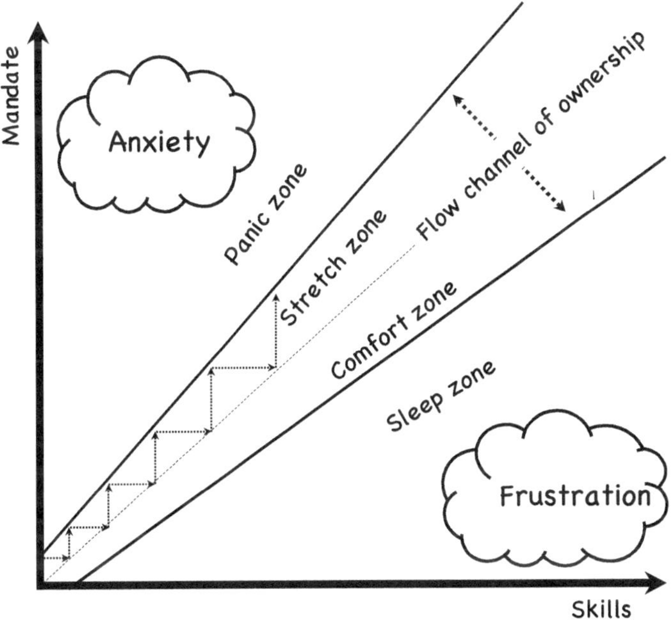

How do you know where a team stands? Team members will also differ in their skills; how do you measure that? I tend to use Management 3.0's Delegation Poker as a means of establishing what mandate the team can handle, while offering sufficient challenge. Ask the team and the responsible management to meet in a room. Get everyone mixed up, so avoid having the management on one side and the team on the other. Make it clear that everyone's opinion is equally important. Explain how Delegation Poker works, and ask all attendees to discuss and determine the topics for which they want to discuss the mandate. For example, who is in charge of recruiting new team members? Delegation Poker applies seven mandates to this end:

1. The management decides and does not discuss this with the Team.
2. The management decides and explains to the team why they have made this decision.
3. The management decides, but only after consulting the team.
4. The management and the team decide with an equal vote.
5. The team decides, but only after consulting the management.
6. The team decides and explains the reasons for their decision to the management.
7. The team decides and does not discuss this with the management.

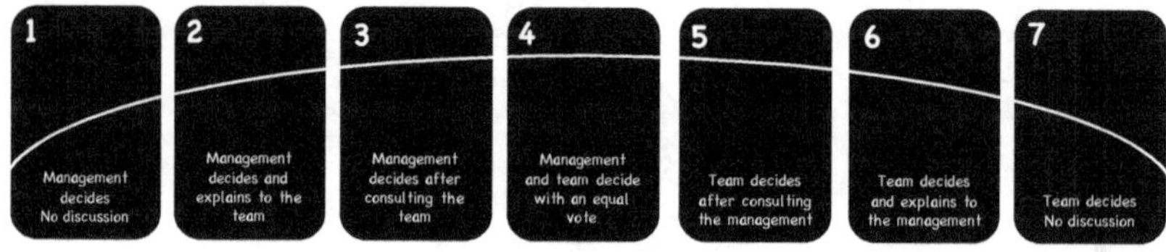

Once the items have been determined, the agile coach facilitates a socio-cratic process. He starts by discussing the interpretation of the topic. Are we all on the same page about this? Do we have practical examples? Once everyone agrees on the interpretation of the topic, the agile coach asks all attendees to choose a card and not show it yet. When everyone has chosen, the attendees show their card. When playing poker as a working method, we always ask the outliers about their arguments, with the utmost respect. Their arguments often contain knowledge that has not yet been shared in the group, but which is relevant for arriving at the best decision. In other words, if the majority of the attendees choose 3, and one person chooses 7, and one person chooses 1, the arguments for 7 and 1 will be the most interesting ones to discuss. Once the outliers have stated their opinion, ask if anyone wishes to share an argument why 3 is the best option after all. This ensures that all the arguments are presented in a balanced way. There is no discussion at this stage, just listening. It is striking to see that the management often offers a higher mandate than team members ask for. This comes from the false perception teams hold that the management wants to keep all mandates. The management, on the other hand, wants teams to take their responsibility, in other words, to take the mandate.

The greatest value of this poker session is in the dialogue between the management and the team. They will start to understand each other on topics that are usually not mutually discussed, or much too little. The second highest value is that the dialogue shows where the team currently stands. Which mandate would be a challenging experiment for them? Yes, you read that right. The session does not result in a fixed mandate, but an experiment. We're going to see how things work out in practice when the team is given this mandate. It is important to remember this when we play poker again after the opinion-forming process, in order to make decisions. Once again, you ask everyone to choose a card. Now we start an open discussion about a mandate that is challenging but won't cause damage. A trained agile coach will also make this assessment and guide toward a challenging mandate, which he expects to be just about within the flow channel. Pay particular attention to the team's choice here. They will never poker themselves out of the flow channel. This gives you certainty about what is within the flow channel. At the end of the session, you end up with a matrix with the items and the chosen mandates. The team puts it up on the wall in the team room, so that the mandate of this team is clear for all to see. They can also hold each other accountable for this, both within the team and between the management and the team.

	1	2	3	4	5	6	7
team formation					X		
workplace							X
dev. tools						X	
holidays							X
themes				X			
epics					X		
features						X	
... ...						X	

As soon as the management or someone in the team notices in practice that the mandate is not working optimally, the team and the management reconvene at the first request, and play the item again. The team may be given a smaller or a larger mandate. Please note, this choice is another experiment, until someone thinks it can be done better. In this regard, the mandate is highly dynamic. The agile coach checks whether the team's mandate grows over the coming months, quarters or years. If it does, all is well. If not, there's probably something going on and you will need to investigate.

Holistic performance

If a team starts to perform better, that is great. But if this does not improve the organization as a whole, you end up with a negative balance. Being part of a winning team is addictive. You don't want to lose that feeling. Make sure that the team does not unknowingly start using the 'win-lose' pattern. We all unconsciously carry that pattern with us, because we created it in our brains when we played games as children. Many games can be won by making sure the other person loses. Teams unconsciously use this pattern in our brains to be the winning team in the organization. Without meaning harm, they risk becoming the mole in the organization that makes sure that others are worse. Make the winning teams aware of this pattern and discuss how they can be an integral part of the winning organization as a whole. Not by undermining their competitors, but by being more valuable to the end users, by delighting customers! You need the entire organization, you won't be able to achieve this with your team alone.

The role of the agile coach in the development of an agile team

If the agile team is a scrum team with a scrum master, I usually assume the role of the agile organization coach, and I become the agile coach for the board and the management. The scrum master is then the agile coach for the team, and I keep my distance on purpose. In this case, my role is to coach-the-coach, for the scrum master and the product owner. Having two agile coaches working on the same team simultaneously is not useful for the team nor the agile coach. Sure, it sounds like fun and two heads are better than one, but in practice the agile coach is often more experienced and he may subconsciously quickly undermine the scrum master's position. It is better to work on the team's next step via the scrum master than directly. If the team does not have a scrum master, I am also the agile coach for the team.

How does this work?

The flow of a team coach session looks like this:

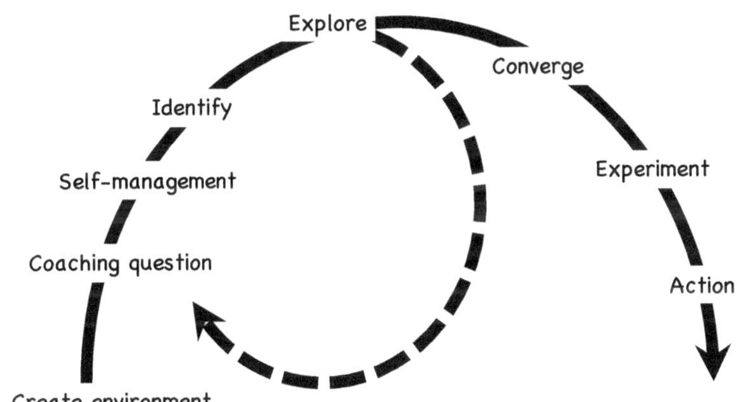

Create a safe environment

Don't start before you have created a safe environment. If there is no natural safe environment yet, you should create one temporarily. This starts with the relationship between the agile coach and the team. Does the team know who you are, what your agenda is, and whether they can trust you? Spend time on these questions. Make sure that they know a lot about you. Your strongest point is that you do not show your strongest points, but position yourself on an equal footing with the team, and are not afraid to show your vulnerable side. This creates a safe climate in which team members are not afraid to show their vulnerable side either. We inherently put more trust in people about whom we know a lot, than people about whom we know little. Make sure they can read you by being open and transparent about your intentions. Show that you are not there to judge or tell them what to do. Make it clear that you are there to support the team on the team's agenda, and only if the team wants you to. Show interest in the team and ask what they are struggling with or want help with. Acknowledge any accompanying emotions, but don't sit and cry with them. They do not need someone who cries with them, but someone who can create the solutions with them. Show that the choice is not up to you but to the team. Ask informative and powerful questions to understand context, activate their thinking, and spur them into action. Challenge them to try things out.

If the work environment does not feel safe, organize a safe environment in which the judging or judgmental people are not present, for example, by sitting in a confined space with the team and discussing the Vegas Rule with them. The Vegas Rule states: "what happens in Vegas, stays in Vegas." Only at a later stage, when the team experiences more team safety, will they reject this rule of their own accord. The Vegas Rule usually only applies during one or two sessions with the teams I have coached. If a session takes place online, do not record it. Do not betray their trust, in other words: do not say anything about this session outside the team. An agile coach who no longer has the team's confidence should go home.

Discover the coaching question

The coaching question is the team's actual request for help. It is often a reason that underlies symptoms that people know how to express. For example, the team members may not experience it as useful when they have seven sprint goals and these are defined almost on an individual level. And during the daily scrum, they do not experience much value when the back-end developer shares all the technical details that no one else understands. Maybe they don't think refinement is going well. In that case, the coaching question is not to emphasize why a sprint goal and a daily are important, or to practice with this. Symptom control rarely yields results. The trick is to discuss this and discover what would really help the team. As an example, I recently discovered, in a team with the symptoms mentioned above, that the focus of their dialogues had shifted from value to work over time. They were barely talking about value anymore, but mainly about the work. To them, it made sense that their work delivered value, as they had already proven this. They were missing the common thread, however, and had started to adopt a sense of every man for himself. The underlying coaching question here is to help the team to be able once more to base their thinking on value. It's fine if this involves products and technology as well, of course, but the common thread should be the value for the intended end user! I asked questions about what happened to the value, and what was the value of what the team came up with in the sprint. I also asked them how the product owner talked about this, what they were doing as a team, and what the yield might be if they started using value as the common thread. The product owner and the team went to work on it, and the energy visibly returned. All of a sudden, they were all back on the same page.

Self-management

To arrive at the underlying coaching question, you need to go through several steps. It is important to realize that the symptoms the team mentions also trigger an emotional reaction in you, the agile coach. You once taught the team members the essence of the daily scrum, and now they are reading their schedules out loud to each other. You may find yourself thinking: "Will they ever learn? Didn't we spend entire sessions on making the values explicit? Did they think we were doing this for the fun of it?" If this happens, start by listening to the arguments your 'patient and relativizing self' puts forward, so that your 'fast' and your 'a lick and a promise' selves don't disrupt the team's process.

Identify

Once you've put your patient and relativizing self in charge, you can facilitate a group dialogue. You can use games for this purpose, such as the team health check. But you can also ask informative questions about exactly how they do things, what exactly is happening, and how they feel about it. Start by asking about the context and slowly but surely work your way to questions about the core of the matter. What is the essence of the daily for the team? What is the use of a sprint goal to the team? When do they do a refinement, who initiates it, and who takes the lead? What do they discuss then, and how does this help the team?

Listening on three levels

There are three ways to listen.

1. Listening internally: at this level, you listen mostly to what you expect to be said. When you ask questions, you do so mainly because you want to confirm your own ideas. This results in selective perception. which doesn't add much. After all, you hear what you want to hear, and you already knew that.

2. Focused listening: at this level, your listening is free from judgment and respectful of what the other person is saying. Don't think in terms of good or bad, and don't try to help straight away. You are sincerely interested in the other person's opinion. You hear what they are saying and you ask questions to make sure you have understood them correctly.

3. Global listening: You are interested in what happens to the group dynamics when people are talking to each other. What is happening in the group is more important to you than your personal opinion, or what the individuals are saying.

Level one interferes with good collaboration. As an agile coach you listen from level two, but mainly and actively on level three. You will also benefit greatly if agile teams can listen at levels two and three. So, teach agile teams about the three levels and also coach them in focused and global listening.

Exploring

Now try to discover, through questions, what will help the team. You can do this with questions that get the team's thinking process going: powerful questions that put the team in motion. You could ask things like:

"What is the true value you deliver in that sprint?" If they answer with a list of tasks, ask "What's the use to your end user?" This will slowly but surely turn the team's focus to the values. Next, ask them how value is discussed in the refinement sessions, part 1 of the planning session, the daily, and in the reviews. If these sessions don't start with a real sense of what value the team is creating for whom, the coaching question will be to help the team change from a work crew into a value-generating unit.

Now that the real coaching question has come into view, it is once again important to keep an eye on your self-management. Which 'self' can be allowed to sit next to the driver? And which 'self' might obstruct this phase?

Continue to alternate informative and powerful questions and experience how the team is gaining more insight into what is happening. Use cause-and-effect visualizations where possible to provide insight into how their system is currently working, and how it might work.

Converge

Discuss what the team could do, and prioritize what will help the team the most. Don't strive to get all the actions onto to-do lists. Two or three actions are generally enough to initiate the desired movement. Even a single action is progress. This will help the team more than a long to-do list that never budges because it is simply too much and too diffuse.

Experiment

Think of the agreed action in terms of an experiment, in other words: we're not sure yet whether it is the best action, but we are doing it so we can learn from it. Therefore, agree on a follow-up moment to discuss the experiment. Share what people have learned from it, and agree on the next experiment to continue growing along the same path.

Consent

Not all team members need to agree unanimously on the experiment to be performed. In many cases, full support and commitment only come about once you are successful. And when you start something new, you are not yet successful. So, do not strive for a false basis, to avoid creating a false reality. What you do need is consent, in other words: team members will consent if they expect the experiment not to cause any damage. So, we do it, unless someone has serious objections on the grounds that it could cause damage. Of course, this should not be used as a veto, in which case the objection is not valid.

Reconvene within a month, review what has been learned and work your way through the flow of a team coaching session again.

How agile teams improve themselves

An agile coach will regularly be tempted to intervene immediately if they see something that could be improved. He may think some swift action is in order. This is not an effective way to grow teams, however. Agile teams first and foremost improve themselves. Where this is not yet the case, the agile coach can help with everything a team needs to improve itself.

Agile teams regularly convene for a retrospective session. This usually takes only half an hour, which can be plenty of time to get the team thinking about what is going well and what can be improved. Please note, it is always about self-improvement. In other words, what could the team do better? They share the successes in the same session to create a balanced atmosphere and because their awareness of the successes should not be lost. The improvements may even include items that are going well, but which the team will probably be able to improve. The team chooses what they are going to improve and which team member is to take action to this end. The agile coach only comes in if the team doesn't pick up a next improvement of its own accord. You can rest assured that even with the best agile teams, this moment returns regularly, so you will never be out of work.

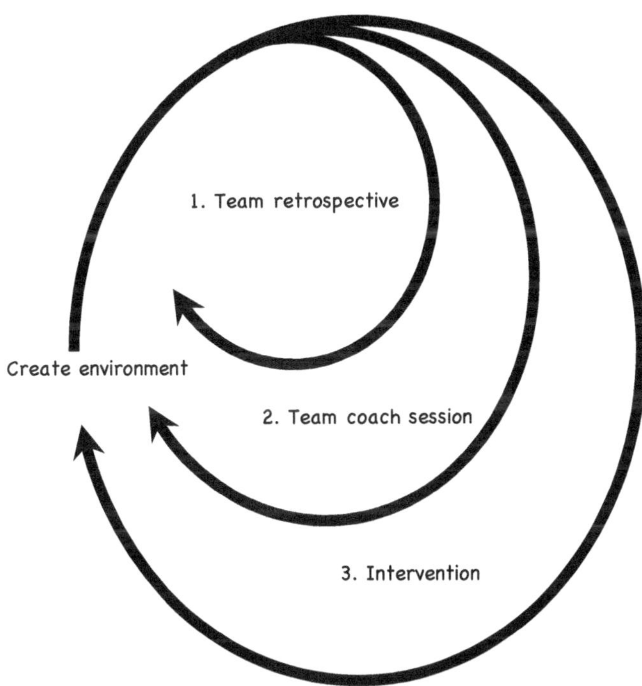

Integral agile coaching model

Over the years, I have used many models that support the agile coach: clever models and frameworks that can help to solve a piece of the puzzle each time. I have integrated a few models, to make it easier to see the entire puzzle. After all, a chain is only as strong as its weakest link. Before you know it, you will be coaching people without awareness, knowledge and experience, or give immature teams the full mandate. Plenty of pitfalls, particularly in the storming phase, when many people call for a return to the peace and quiet of yesteryear

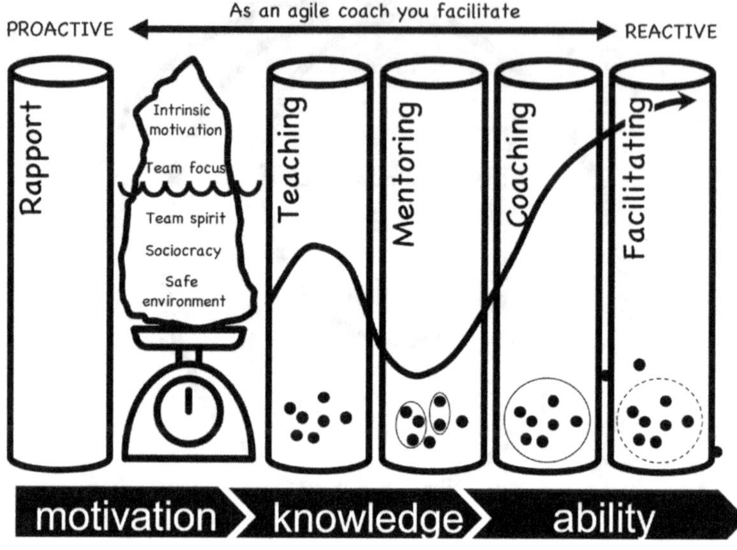

The model has five cylinders that can be filled, just like a savings campaign. When one cylinder is sufficiently filled (it does not have to be completely full), you can already move on to the next cylinder with new challenges. The agile coach plays a different role in each phase. To start with, this role is highly proactive, and as time goes on it turns into a more reactive role.

The model starts with rapport; this is coaching jargon for connection. In order to be able to create rapport, first of all you need to have synchronized your own thoughts, feelings, and behavior. In other words, do these form a continuous whole inside yourself, or is there a difference between your thoughts and your behavior? If you create a rapport with yourself, you will become an authentic personality who quickly wins the trust of the people with whom you are in contact. The next step is to tie in with the thoughts, feelings, and behavior of the person with whom you want to create rapport. You create a safe environment in which everything can be said and you try to connect with where the agile team stands at that moment. Particularly in the beginning, you may find you thoroughly disagree with each other, but you don't want to start as two opposing parties. Rapport does not mean that you have to agree with each other, in other words. Rapport involves understanding, recognition of the situation, recognition of the team members' feelings and acceptance of your own feelings. It means respecting that you are all different and finding out where your similarities lie, in order to have a shared starting point. You can achieve this by synchronizing your thoughts, feelings, and behavior. In neuroscience, this is called mirroring. It can be verbal or non-verbal. Connect on the language and behavior level, so that you tune in to the team's rhythm and energy. Look for those places where you can join the different team members, where you have that magic 'click' with each other. You need that click if you are embarking on a long journey with the entire team. You can start that journey when you share the same starting point. If you respect the differences at the point of departure, you will also be rewarded with respect.

Practice creating rapport, particularly with people with whom you have absolutely no click. If you manage to embark on a journey with them, you will really get the hang of it!

The integral agile coaching model also has a scale, on which the agile coach weighs what is already present in the team and what can still be added. The scale is positioned between the Rapport and Teaching cylinders. Only people who want to are able to learn new things and be coached.

We have already discussed the Knowledge and Ability phases. Here, you can also see the maturity stages and the curve from Tuckman's high-performing team model reflected in the agile coaching model.

The model is not intended to be static. You will regularly find that in an M4 team, something can happen that makes you return to 'start' again. M4 teams do not remain M4 teams without effort, so use the integral agile coaching model particularly for the required maintenance.

Remote agile coaching

Not all teams have the luxury of being able to sit together at the same location. Distributed agile teams have been assembled with the best professionals from all around the world. These are usually the heavyweights among the professionals, who are also perfectly able to work together virtually. Their life happens in the cloud and virtual meetings are the standard for them.

As a result of Covid-19, many agile teams have suddenly become distributed teams as well. These are not necessarily the same heavyweights, and they suddenly find themselves working from home involuntarily, with their partner working at the same kitchen table and the children reluctantly doing their homework. This new reality requires some attention for how to organize this properly and how to fulfill your role as an agile coach remotely.

What are the benefits of working as a remote team?
- Less time spent commuting, and no travel stress.
- People are more creative when they are ungroomed in their dressing gown.
- Fewer disruptive factors from within the team or organization.

What is missing for remote teams?
- Valuable cross-pollination that is unnoticeable when you work together in the same space.
- Having a quick chat.
- Putting shared information on a dynamic wall.
- Sensing each other because you are together.
- Team dynamics.
- A natural sense of belonging.
- Creativity (decreases before your very eyes).
- Team members become task-oriented.

In the short term, an increase in productivity is noticeable, because team members start to work in a more task-oriented manner, based on the creativity they had when they were still together. However, this is a short-term upturn that is quickly lost because team spirit and creativity decrease when team members work separately for longer periods.

What are the benefits for the remote agile coach?
- Faster contact with the entire or partial team.
- Online whiteboard sessions are automatically recorded digitally, so they can be easily continued the next time.

What does the remote agile coach miss?
- It is more difficult to observe the team properly.
- Significantly reduced non-verbal communication.
- There is less to learn from team dynamics.
- There is no physical work space for creativity.

The agile coach no longer sees the complete reality. Observing the actual team dynamics is no longer possible, you have to make do with snapshots of the occasional online session.

How do you deal with this?
Buy the biggest screen with the best resolution you can find that fits your PC or laptop. You are going to want to see the team members as large as possible so you can perceive emotions. And you will want to be able to see all the members of a team at the same time, so that you can also observe some team dynamics.

Introduce some specific good practices that are associated with online team sessions:
1. Sessions are never longer than 3 consecutive hours. This is already quite long. A maximum of one hour is preferable, but for knowledge sessions, for example, you may need more consecutive time.
2. Agree that everyone turns on their camera. Non-verbal communication is crucial.

3. Take a break of at least ten minutes every hour. The team members should be moving around during this break and not look at their screens. Many teams plan the review, retro and planning sessions for the same day. In that case, schedule a short break between these events and agree that the participants will step away from their screen.

4. Staring at a screen for too long is very bad for your eyes, which is why remote agile teams apply the '20-20 rule'. Every twenty minutes, the participants look away from their screens for twenty seconds at something as far away from their eyes as possible, for example, looking out the window into the distance.

5. Do not interrupt each other. If you want to say something, raise your (virtual) hand.

6. Use virtual breakout rooms and online whiteboards to keep the sessions lively for everyone.

7. Do not make an unannounced video recording of the session. Preferably don't video record at all as doing so may prevent team members from speaking freely. Moreover, recordings rarely prove valuable in practice, viewing them later on is a waste of time.

Suggest that in addition to the formal events, the teams also organize social events, like an online Friday afternoon drinks session. This is, of course, voluntary, but so much fun that everyone will probably want to be there. Combine this with a quiz or karaoke, for example. Maybe someone can play the guitar or piano? Make a silly effort to play requests from the team as a virtual occasion band. Play an online game with a competitive element, which continues the following Friday. Or maybe a team member wants to give a virtual tour of their home. Some agile teams end each day together with half an hour of social time whenever they work from home. Use these social online events to help the team members to get to know the people behind their colleagues better. This contributes to team safety, as a result of which they will also collaborate more transparently at work and dare to share and discuss more.

Hybrid teams

Not every organization will be able to do this, but you could try to organize some agile events in the open air, such as the retrospective and the first part of the planning session. A team could meet in a garden or a park to do this on an afternoon. Even if they have to keep a six-foot distance in times of a pandemic, these events are easy to organize. You could finish the event with a meal: distanced, but still together.

Another option would be for two or three team members to get together in the physical team room if they want to pursue or create something together. This could be for a half or an entire day, depending on the requirements.

Digitally together

My children came up with a surprising solution during the pandemic. They, too, missed being together in class or during breaks at school. Inventive as they are, the kids started doing their homework on the iPad or laptop with Facetime running via the Wi-Fi. They created a continuous visual connection with classmates who were also doing homework. When I first saw my kids doing this, I was surprised and asked what they were doing. "Oh, you know, just doing homework." I said "But you're not even talking." My daughter replied: "I know, But it's just nicer like this." The next day, I shared this anecdote with one of the teams I coach. I knew they were missing the sense of connection now that they were working from home. Three front-end developers subsequently adopted this habit and are now virtually in the same room every day. Other team members do the same from time to time. When they have a question, rather than having to get in touch, just like in the agile team space, they simply raise their heads, look at the teammates who are virtually working next to them and ask their question. Their teammates do the same, as they would in the physical team space: they either respond or leave it to another team member. Try experimenting with this. I can't give you practical examples as yet of teams imitating physical space with multiple cameras and monitors, but I guess that's only a matter of time.

PHASE 4: DEVELOP YOURSELF INTO AN EXPERT

Once you feel comfortable as a scrum master or with agile coaching at team level, it is time to challenge yourself again in the stretch zone to become an expert. I don't know any agile coaches who are an expert in every area, and frankly, I think that's impossible. To reach expert status, you develop professional depth in one or two sub-areas of Agile Delivery and/or Business Agility. Possible examples include:

Agile Delivery
1. Enterprise Product Ownership
2. Delivery Management
3. Agile Engineering
4. Agile Testing
5. DevOps
6. Agile Expert Coaching

Business Agility
1. Agile Leadership
2. Adaptive Strategy
3. Adaptive Organization Design
4. Agile Marketing
5. Agile HR
6. Agile Transition

Soft Skills
1. Emotional Intelligence

2. Work/Life coach
3. NLP

The idea is to develop yourself to the highest level in at least one sub-area. Your aim is to transcend this level with innovative insights that also allow the agile community to grow. This takes you to places where you would otherwise never go, both among colleagues and in organizations. You conduct dialogues that will also take you to a higher level as a generic agile coach.

Preferably choose a development direction in which you are already at an advantage with your experience. After all, you want to be able to transcend the highest level and treat the world to your innovative insights. I originally started my career in database marketing; this gave me the advantage of having experienced how we can learn and improve based on empirical data. I'm a marketer who believes in pull marketing: this means your target group knows where to find you because you deliver the best value for the customer. Rather than investing in advertisements and salespeople, you invest in smart communication and the optimization of the best value for the customer. This background has allowed me to specialize in agile marketing. Part of that specialization was writing my book Agile Marketing in 2016. After all, experts have a desire to treat the world to wonderful new insights. The dialogues that such a book evokes, also allow you to grow as an expert. And in turn, your value to the world increases, too. Sharing is growing.

I have been active as an agile coach since 2010, mainly on the business side. I wrote this book as part of my development in agile expert coaching. You, too, can choose in which field you want to become an expert. Experts tend to have better access to coach the organization because they have proven that they can acquire, transcend, and share in-depth knowledge and expertise.

In the expert phase, you make your knowledge transferable, for example, by giving presentations or training courses about the agile mindset or methodology. Write articles and post blogs, vlogs, and tutorials. Doing so will force your brain to transfer the huge amount of knowledge and experience that you have acquired over time.

In the expert phase, you will also start to engage in dialogues with more stakeholders outside the team. Or you may facilitate several teams simultaneously. Dimensions are added at the program or organizational level, allowing you to grow.

PHASE 5: COACHING THE AGILE ORGANIZATION

As an agile coach, you also have a role to play in the development of the agile organization. This chapter offers an impression of what an agile organization is, and how it is different from traditional organizations.

After at least two centuries of running organizations like a machine, we sauntered into a new era around the turn of the millennium. We can no longer maintain organizations like a machine in a time that requires rapid adjustment, and when organizations are becoming increasingly complex. We now live in an era in which organizations change back from a machine into an organic system and find their way in an evolutionary fashion. This paradigm shift for organizations will be completed in the first half of the 21st century. Agile coaches play a crucial role in this transition.

Frederic Laloux spent three years researching contemporary leading organizations in highly diverse sectors and countries. These organizations perform significantly better than traditional, machine-oriented organizations – not only below the line, but particularly above it. He describes what emerged as the Cyane organization. And although Laloux does not call it the agile organization in so many words, I did recognize all the characteristics of the flexible agile organization, including the evolutive goal. They are organic environments where people are free to be themselves again and feel valuable and happy. Where power is arranged laterally and in self-organization, and where everyone can feel the deeper meaning. And where both the individual and the bigger picture can thrive. It turns out that these are the organizations that are the most valuable to their customers, employees, shareholders, and the world. One example of a Cyane organization success story is Buurtzorg, which was founded in 2006 by district nurse Jos de Blok and has quickly grown into the most valuable player in the sector. They provide fantastic care and a wonderful workplace, in a sector where both of these elements have been under pressure for years. So, what's holding us back? Why can't every healthcare organization be a Cyane organization?

Characteristics of successful agile organizations

How do you recognize an agile organization? It is a flexible organization that is consistently the first to successfully adapt to the changing environment. The one that enjoys being one step ahead of change, and in doing so drives the change. Small organizations are inherently better at this than large ones. In large organizations, habits have often become institutionalized. In other words: the organizational culture cherishes successful habits from the past because they experience them as safe. Okay, so they are patterns that have become part of the culture of an organization. This actually creates an opportunity to create agile habits in the organization that still feel safe and familiar to employees. Going along with the change, consciously innovating every time, not holding on to what is but to what is to come, can also be good habits that ensure success. And they can also evolve into a pattern that takes root in the culture of an organization. I am hopeful that this will happen in many companies in the next few decades. Agile organizations live based on the belief that nothing is permanent, except change. If they don't change sufficiently, they become nervous and insecure, rather than becoming nervous and insecure about the change itself.

Nokia was one of the most innovative organizations in the world, which brought them great success. Having started out supplying rubber boots for hunters, they discovered the need for their customers to have better rubber tires under their jeeps, to increase grip on soggy surfaces. They started developing these tires together with their users. When they noticed the hunters' need to communicate with each other in the woods, it formed the basis for developing a specific mobile phone: one that could withstand rough handling and had a long battery life. However, these phones became such a huge success worldwide that Nokia lost their agility. And even though they were the most innovative organization, with a global market share that exceeded their three largest competitors combined, they found themselves out of the market within a year of the iPhone being introduced. They were unable to adapt to the change quickly enough.

Apple was founded in 1976 by Steve Jobs, Steve Wozniak and Ronald Wayne. Thanks to their distinctive value proposition, they managed to conquer a large share of the market, especially with the Apple I, the first small personal computers at the time. However, Steve Jobs, a value thinker pur sang, was expelled from the company because he was too stubborn to be at the shareholders' beck and call. The shareholders demanded more focus on turnover, profit, and cost savings and felt that Jobs was nowhere near commercial enough. Apple's popularity declined and competitors caught up with Apple thanks to better value propositions. In 1997, Apple came close to bankruptcy. They were saved by competitor Microsoft with a $150 million investment. The only reason Microsoft dared to make this investment was because Jobs returned to the company. Since then, Apple has returned to its focus on delivering the highest value rather than selling products. As a result, they are making fantastic products that sell extremely well.

The biggest challenge is to keep things agile while the organization is successful and growing to a larger scale. The organization must be willing, hungry even, to replace anything that has proven successful with something else that is not yet successful with anyone. The insatiable drive to work continuously with the unpredictable is the most important characteristic of the agile organization. Amazon is another example: next-day delivery before 11:00 a.m. is not enough for them. As soon as they realized that consumers really want their delivery at the time of the order, they started looking at options for immediate delivery. This led them to experiment with drones that start flying as soon as someone orders something, as early as 2016. In doing so, they are learning about what their future may look like. They are continuously stretching their comfort zone to see what is possible when they color outside existing lines. Coolblue, a Dutch e-commerce company that sells tech products, has been delivering on Sundays for a while now, with many deliveries made by bike. Their motto, 'Anything for a smile', forces them to constantly come up with something new to surprise their customers. Today's customer delighter (a positive surprise that is valuable to your customers) can quickly become tomorrow's mere hygiene maintenance (if you can't deliver it, you are kicked out of the market). Online shops with a slow delivery process or complicated return procedure lose out to organizations that try to beat their own, already winning, process with an even better customer delight process.

In typical agile organizations, revolutionary ideas are created by the people who enjoy this process. They derive pleasure and satisfaction from surprising users with valuable things. Agile teams are given sufficient space to discover new things and learn from experiments. This is how they grow to their full potential, and the organization grows along with them.

What can agile coaches contribute to this process? What should you pay attention to in order to estimate the next step in the development toward an agile organization?

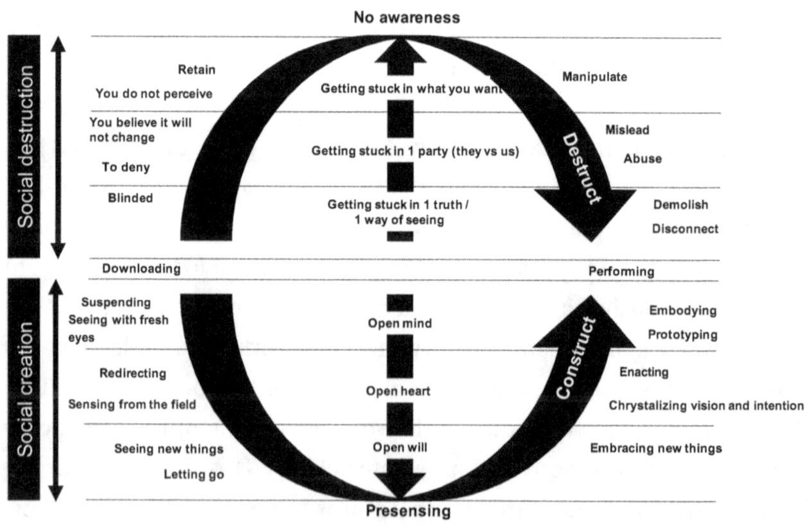

Old patterns often need to be broken and new beliefs born in order for the agile organization to emerge. I usually work based on my free interpretation of Otto Scharmer's Theory U, examining the following characteristics in the organization that, combined, make the change possible.

From a fixed mindset to a growth mindset

People with a fixed mindset have fixed beliefs and see changes as a threat, as opposed to people with a growth mindset, who assume that their beliefs can grow as they increase their experience and learning. They see change as a good, and even necessary, thing. People with a fixed mindset believe that they are either good at something or not: it is black or white. Those with a growth mindset, on the other hand, are convinced that they can learn anything as long as they want to. People with a fixed mindset see feedback as a personal accusation, and if they fail they see it as something that is bad. With a growth mindset, people tend to see feedback as constructive, and welcome failure as a learning opportunity. Agile organizations need people with a growth mindset.

What should an agile coach do in an organization where a lot of people have a fixed mindset? Well, this is going to make a transition a little more challenging. People with a fixed mindset can change, but they need to see the benefit and value of a growth mindset before they believe it. That is why organizations always need a few people in their own ranks with a growth mindset. They are living proof to the fixed mindset camp that it is safe for them too to believe and see new opportunities. When people with a fixed mindset see living proof in their own organization, they will be able to adjust their own beliefs. It takes time, but it can be done. Organize dialogue sessions, mainly with middle managers, about fixed and growth mindsets. Ask what they understand these concepts to mean, what they think is desirable, and how they might encourage this in their organization. Coach proactively in practice so that they can model a growth mindset for the rest of the organization. I have noticed that if middle management does this, you will quickly reach the required critical mass of 50% with a growth mindset. Do not sit around waiting for this to happen, but continue to develop the organization simultaneously. The transition will start to gain momentum if you start making progress on several fronts at the same time.

From the visionary leader to the mental model of your organization

Considering all the above, how do you see the beliefs and convictions in your organization? Has only the leader adopted them, or the people who deliver value, or all of them? Are you clinging to old successful patterns, or do you constantly challenge yourselves to step outside your comfort zone? Do you respect outliers and do you prefer to hire people who think differently than is customary in your organization? Or do you prefer people with the same views, and do you try to convince people with a different opinion of your own opinion and facts from the past? Tough question, isn't it? No one said developing an agile organization would be easy. But once the agile organization gets under way, it can make everyone's contribution to that organization so much easier. People who think differently will suddenly turn out to add high value because you deal with them differently. You discover things that you would otherwise only have found logical after your competitors have already achieved success with them.

What should the agile coach do if the vision mainly comes from the leader and not the people who deliver the value? There is an important task here to work on a shared vision of what value constitutes.

Explain to the team what the difference is between the product and the value, as I described earlier in this book. Allow the teams to work out for themselves what value they deliver for whom; this will result in a wealth of great insights into potential user needs. Teach the product owner to prioritize these user stories in a Value / Effort matrix, and how to convert them into a development strategy. Next, make the connection by inviting the leader (s) of the organization to join the teams, and facilitate a lively dialogue about what they see as value and why they have set certain priorities in their development strategy. Rather than the visionary leaders trying to convince the creators, the convictions are now driven from the bottom up and explained in a development strategy. What starts to emerge here is a beautiful thing to behold: it's as if another 'self' has taken over in the leaders' driver seat. They will be over the moon about finally having the dialogue they always wanted, but never had because the vision was always fed bottom-down.

From vertical to horizontal

The pigeonholing that is sometimes prevalent in hierarchies stimulates so-called vertical thinking. This is also known as the silo mentality. This way of thinking and working became popular during the industrial age, in production environments with predictable processes. The 'what' and 'how' are completely fixed in this setting. In these environments, the silos and pigeonholes have proven their functionality with respect to easy upscaling. Based on economies of scale, the organization can then reduce the costs per unit and thus significantly increase the profit margin. Creativity is not desired in this setting, as it leads to unnecessary discussions and wasting valuable production time. The focus is on hard work here.

But what do you do as an agile coach if your teams' task is not a predictable production process? What if their tasks involve organizational, product, proposition, customer, or communication development, in other words, everything that has to do with development, is changeable, or related to unpredictability? What if an effective journey of discovery delivers value? In these cases, there is suddenly a lot of interdependency with the rest of the organization, and the silos stand in the way of creating new value together. Rather than vertically, you will want to move horizontally through the organization, exactly in the same way the value is delivered to the end user. These value streams always pass horizontally through the operational layer of the organization. There is no such thing as vertical value streams. If you want to stimulate the horizontal value stream, it is useful to also set up the organization horizontally. And to facilitate the value creation process with the customer or user and the horizontal value stream in the middle and everything else around it.

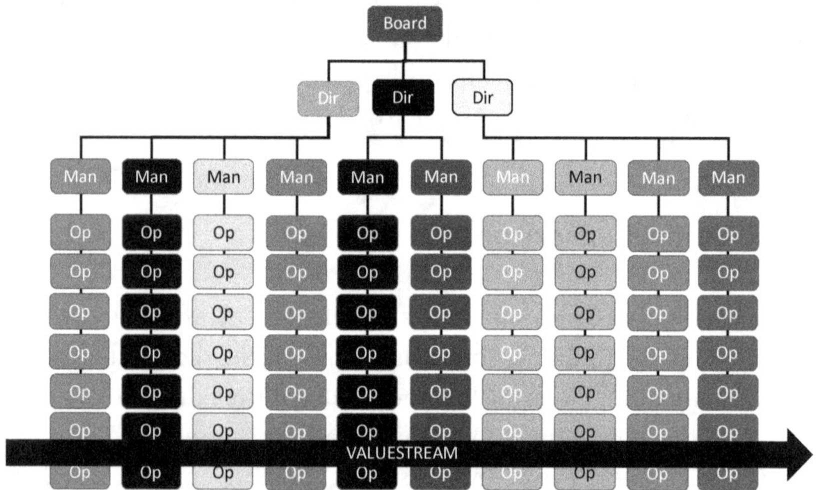

From departments to a blended organization

Traditional organizations are divided into departments, such as the IT department, marketing department, communication department, sales department and so on. Every department has its own manager, with their own management style, ambitions, and objectives. The advantage of having departments is that all the professionals are in one place and can therefore tackle big jobs together. They speak the same lingo and are cast in the same mold as far as their profession is concerned, so they tend to be of the same mind. There is a natural cross-pollination that ensures that employees can continue to develop in the workplace. It is clear who is responsible for communication, for example, and the communication budget is also easy to monitor in this way. Nevertheless, in an agile environment, traditional departments have major drawbacks. Using the same example, the communication department cannot ensure a good market position for the organization all by itself. There is a certain dependence on the other departments to ultimately deliver the value in the market. And the organization only has a raison d'être, turnover, profits, and market share if it delivers value in the market. If the organization delivers better value than the other providers, its raison d'être, turnover, profit, and market share will grow. And in the current market rhythm, an organization will need to be able to do this ever faster, without loss costs or damage to its reputation. Being able to deliver positively distinctive new values quickly has become essential – my previous book Agile Marketing is entirely devoted to this topic. A well-functioning department is not enough to achieve this. Managers who primarily want to ensure that their department is running smoothly or that they are a good manager do not focus on delivering new value to end users ever faster. Employees who focus on departmental objectives do not focus on the rapid delivery of positively distinctive new value either.

Enter into a dialogue with the board, HR, and management. Organize awareness sessions, in which you visualize how the value is taken to customers in silos, and how it could be delivered to them differently. Suggest experimenting in the organization with an autonomous and multi-disciplinary end-to-end team that can handle an entire value stream.

In the agile organization, the development, marketing and optimization of new value propositions is executed by multidisciplinary units. These units are made up of every discipline that is needed to deliver the value proposition. This unit is not managed by (department) managers. I sometimes see that the value-generating unit is expanded with specialists from departments and that the department manager still wants to maintain control over the employee he has 'supplied' or 'lent'. Do not fall into this trap, because this creates units with equal numbers of captains and sailors. This will get you nowhere. The agile value-generating unit should be autonomous and self-organizing in this regard. Preferably, the unit develops toward self-management. The focus is entirely on quickly delivering distinctive values and the necessary rapid learning from real users this requires.

Depending on the intended value proposition, one or more teams are put together with all the disciplines that are needed to develop and deliver the value from start to finish. Front-end, back-end, middleware, product specialists, marketers, communication specialists, and UX designers. In other words: everything that is needed is now present in the unit. You could call it a kind of mini company within the company. When a discipline is needed, we no longer need to negotiate with department managers who have different priorities; we simply take the shortest route to market.

Incidentally, not all the work in the organization is necessarily housed in self-organizing multidisciplinary units. Tasks that have a predictable process and outcome can still be managed by a monodisciplinary department and a department manager. This is true for Coolblue, for example, where most of the work consists of packing, shipping, and invoicing orders as quickly as possible. These are fixed processes with fixed, predictable outcomes. Lean-Six-Sigma delivers more value in this context than Lean-Agile. Dave Snowden's Cynefin framework offers good insights into where which type of work belongs and which leadership style and organizational form are appropriate. Cynefin is a Welsh word that literally translates as 'habitat': it indicates where which work, which people, and which leadership style belong.

The main conclusion from Snowden's research lies at the center of the Cynefin framework: most companies are in a state of 'disorder', or confused about what leadership style they need for what type of work. Most organizations have one dominant leadership style that has become part of the corporate culture and is used for every type of work.

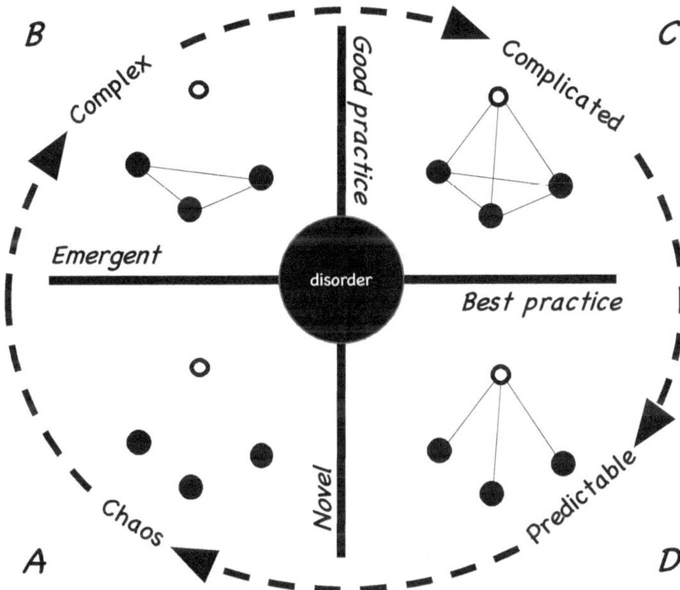

The four quadrants of a blended organization are:

A. Innovations start in chaos

In Dave Snowden's Cynefin leadership framework, this is situated at the bottom left. Only 5% of people are able to recognize new patterns in the changing environment outside of the existing views. But you never know which people in your organization are in that 5% in this particular case. This is why Google asks some of their people to spend 5-10% of their time just doing what they want, rather than their job. This is how they create space to discover new patterns in the chaos of the world.

This is not teamwork and you can't manage it hierarchically, just like you can't manage good moods or creativity hierarchically. It is an integral part of the agile organization which does influence this by creating the right environment in which these eureka moments can happen. This is why agile coaches need to make sure that teams have the space they need to take a broad view. You explain to the management and the teams what the negative consequences are of wanting to do too much work in too little time. Teams should also be careful not to take on too much work, because then they would focus on finishing their work (tunnel vision). Teams that focus on delivering the highest value, on the other hand, need to see new opportunities in order to deliver that value even better, with or without the product they are developing. As an example, a front-end developer at ABN AMRO Bank saw an opportunity to make sharing mutual payments much easier with a combination of a few new technologies. It was the beginning of the so-called Tikkie (Dutch for 'nudge'), which in a short period of time developed into a leading proposition for ABN AMRO Bank, with millions of satisfied users.

Visuospatial thinkers are excellent at discovering promising patterns in a changing environment because they see a context with everything. For verbal thinkers, the first thing that comes to mind when they think of the word 'sheep' would be the letters s-h-e-e-p, and possibly an image of a sheep. Visuospatial thinkers don't see the letters, but a sheep in a flock in a field with a shepherd and a shepherd dog. The shepherd has a long staff, and the dog runs around the flock to keep the sheep together. The sun is shining, but there are also some clouds in the sky, and so on. Visuospatial thinkers can see the entire context from their imagination. However, the difference between visuospatial and verbal thinkers is not black and white, but gray. Word thinkers are also partly visuospatial thinkers, and vice versa. Not everyone is the same, but anyone can have a eureka moment and thus be of great value.

B. Developing new value is complex

Based on newly recognized patterns, the development of a new value carrier is taken to a multidisciplinary agile team, at the top left of the Cynefin framework. This team gets to work to validate the assumptions in the presumptive new value with small, quick, and inexpensive experiments. To this end, they develop pretotypes (pretend as if you have it), prototypes, and minimal viable products. This is teamwork that is preferably not managed hierarchically, because you would miss out on the synergetic effect of the neo-cortexes in the team. A team can quickly experiment and learn in self-organization and with ownership. The team must be able to make quick decisions based on empirical data from observation. Hierarchical management has no added value in this setting; on the contrary, it would unnecessarily hinder this process and only frustrate the team. This complex environment is at the heart of the agile organization.

C. Developing existing values is complicated

New products that prove to be marketable and are introduced to the market, still go through a continuous process of product and process improvements. This part is located at the top right of the Cynefin framework. Anything that has already been validated can be managed centrally, as can most of the daily operations. Continuous improvement, however, requires the same mandate as the agile development teams in the 'Complex' quadrant. The top right quadrant is also still part of the agile organization. You see more and more often that the operational side of the organization is also organized in a completely agile way, with so-called DevOps teams, which take care of both the development and the optimization of the operations.

D. Predictable work is easy

Work that is predictable, for example, a production process with 100% causality, is better managed centrally than in self-organizing agile teams. This work can be found at the bottom right of the Cynefin framework. Process optimization according to Lean-Six-Sigma offers more value here for a stable operation than Lean-Agile.

Here, you will find the activities that are generally easy to automate, which can mean work for agile development or DevOps teams.

From departments to subject and passion groups

So, what if the subject specialists are no longer grouped together in one department, how can they continue to optimize their discipline? Their field is also changing rapidly. Without further training, IT professionals soon lose their value, and marketers and communication specialists also find themselves in an accelerated evolution.

To solve this, introduce subject groups, in which the specialists meet regularly. They can discuss the desired further developments from the point of view of the value-generating units. They prioritize these, and decide, for example, who is going to undertake which training. They also share their knowledge and experience. The subject specialists arrange capacity issues among themselves, across the units. Perhaps there is a temporary need for more capacity in one unit, while in another unit there may temporarily be capacity to spare. The subject groups are self-organizing in the training budget and can be facilitated in this regard by HR or management.

In addition to subject groups, also introduce passion groups. Passion groups are voluntary: anyone can start a passion group and anyone can join in or opt out at any time. A passion group can also dissolve itself. If the passion group has the potential to contribute to the organization, then the organization can make time and budget available to this end. But this is not necessary. It could be a passion group about model airplanes whose members come together in their spare time and bear the costs themselves. It can also be a passion group that delves deeper into nanotechnology, which could be useful for the organization. Managers, canteen employees, IT staff, shareholders, marketers, board members, cleaners and any other employees who take an interest are all welcome to participate. This approach creates a connection across every layer of the organization. The most brilliant (and wild) ideas are born from passion. Passion groups offer people space to grow outside of their existing frameworks. This can lead to enormous value in the organization's culture. It enables new insights to grow into high-profile innovations that will give the organization a future.

From ego to holistic unity

People are more inclined to pursue their personal goals than someone else's. Does that sound reasonable? Maybe it seems logical, but it actually isn't. No one in this world can do it alone, you are always part of the greater whole. Even the likes of Bill Gates and Elon Musk can't do it alone, although it sometimes seems like they can. Incidentally, Microsoft and Tesla can't do it alone, either. Without being part of a larger whole, these brilliant people and organizations are worth nothing. Even an agile team or value-generating unit is worth nothing if it is not part of the bigger whole. A team member alone does not deliver value, the team does not deliver value without the unit, and the unit does not deliver value without the organization, suppliers, and customers. Without the market, the organization can't deliver value, and a sector would die out in a country where substitutes are cheaper or more attractive. As an example, fossil fuel cars are dying a death in Norway, because electric cars are much more attractive there. The government has made them cheaper and attached all kinds of benefits to them, such as being allowed to drive past traffic jams and free parking. A car manufacturer that considers itself a part of the government policy and cultural influences is better able to build a sustainable business than a car manufacturer who thinks its factory is separate from it.

Agile organizations think and work holistically. When making decisions, we start by zooming out to see whether it is the best decision from a holistic perspective. Plans that would cause objectionable damage somewhere in the holistic whole are not executed. If it is not expected to do harm, there is no reason to decline an opportunity to learn and grow.

From fellow countrymen to astronauts

Seeing the Earth from space irreversibly changes astronauts' view of the world. More than ever before, they feel connected to all the people on Earth and become permanently motivated to do the things that preserve life on Earth.

It is an experience that is difficult to put into words. On Christmas Eve 1968, William Anders, an Apollo 8 astronaut, took an unforgettable picture that somewhat captures this experience: a colorful, lush world rising above the sterile, crater-studded lunar horizon. The picture, dubbed 'Earthrise', captured the beauty and fragility of our planet in a single image.

We live in just one of billions of worlds in the Milky Way, but it's the only one within our reach that is just right for human life. Seen from this perspective, the Earth looks enchantingly beautiful. There is really no place in the entire universe like our Earth. NASA astronaut Mike Massimino describes it very aptly: 'I thought at one point, if you could be up in heaven, this is how you would see the planet. And then I dwelled on that and said, no, it's more beautiful than that. This is what heaven must look like. I think of our planet as a paradise. We are very lucky to be here.'

Nearly all astronauts take initiatives for a better world after their career in space. US astronaut Leland Melvin, for example, is working with a coalition of former astronauts to rethink how we can balance environmental health and human needs. They want to encourage the world to adopt a more sustainable lifestyle.

All of us on Earth can learn so much from these astronauts. I wish that from now on, all world leaders would look at Earth from space before they are inaugurated. And that at the start of each summit, they first consider Earthrise, and are fully aware of the greater good, before entering into discussion with each other.

What can agile coaches learn from this? It clearly shows that you will see things differently if you zoom out and consider matters from a broad perspective. Doing so allows you to see how we are all part of a holistic whole in which all the elements react to each other. You will realize that we also depend on this system as a whole for our survival and well-being. Being able to take this viewpoint comes in handy for agile coaches. It would be even better if you can get the management in organizations and agile teams to consider the whole from this perspective. There is a good chance that it will lead to a strong awareness with an intrinsic motivation to develop a healthy organization that adds value. That value doesn't need to be about saving the planet, but it should be about providing value without damaging anyone else.

Use this story in as many group sessions as you can, to raise awareness of the need to think and decide holistically based on the bigger picture. You can put many problems in an organization into perspective with this story. It is also a good story to use as a basis for talking to each other about the meaning of the work.

From managing people to managing the system

You can't change people. People can only change themselves. You can't improve people either. People can only improve themselves. You can, however, develop an organization as an adaptive system, in which people want to change and improve themselves. Managing a system is much more advanced than managing people, however. To do so, you will first of all need an overview of how the different elements in the system interact. This makes organizational coaching an incredibly complex discipline.

Causal loop diagrams are a useful tool for mapping out the interaction between the elements of a system. If you surprise customers, for example, they will order more. More orders will improve the provider's economies of scale and turnover rate. Improved economies of scale allow the provider to buy more cheaply. A better turnover rate considerably lowers the cost per product, which in turn increases profit margins. Thanks to satisfied returning customers, the provider does not need to compete on price and can even increase the selling price. Lower costs and higher returns lead to a significant rise in profit. More profit offers opportunities to invest more… and so on and so forth.

Within the same successful organization, it can happen that a manager gets into an argument with several colleagues, with the result that this manager moves elsewhere and a new manager is hired. The new manager is by definition going to do things differently than his predecessor, simply because the previous manager has been discredited. For example, by focusing on turnover rather than on value, because this causes less discussion and disagreement with colleagues. If the focus is on turnover, there is less attention for innovation, causing turnover growth to slow down. As a result, the manager will tighten the turnover targets and put even more pressure on sales figures, whereby price competition is also enthusiastically pursued. Because the customers feel they are getting more value at the competitor, the turnover subsequently decreases. And so on.

This is why agile coaches see the organization as a system in which all elements interact as described in the previous paragraphs. The agile coach uses the iceberg model as a basis for creating a different system. The iceberg works from the bottom up. A system arises from the collective mental model of the organization, in other words, the things you collectively believe in. For example, the belief that you will achieve more with a focus on value than with a focus on turnover and profit.

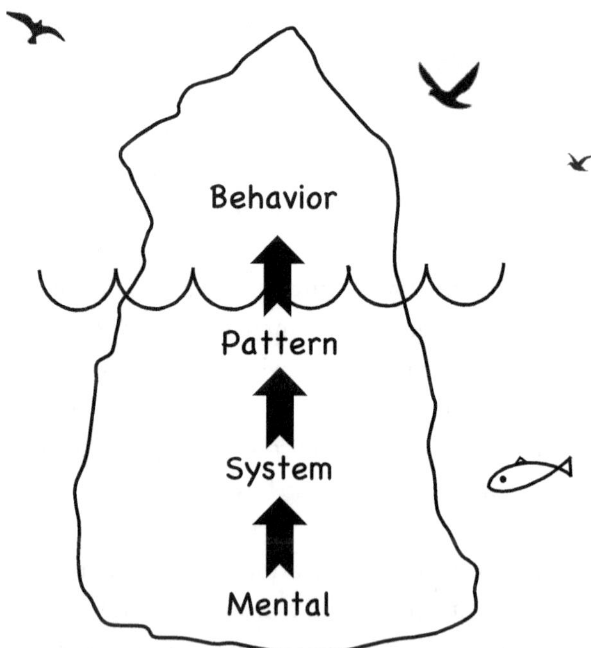

People create this conviction by consciously entering into a dialogue about this, and keeping it alive with (preferably your own) practical examples. The stronger and longer this conviction lives in the organization, the clearer the structure that will arise in the organization that makes it possible to act in accordance with the conviction. As soon as these become repetitive patterns that no one is required to think about anymore, a different culture with matching behaviors arises. When this happens, people no longer change their behavior because the boss wants them to, but because to them it makes sense, and they experience the benefits every day.

From the limbic system to the neo-cortex

People tend to react from the limbic system in their brains, which is ruled by all the routine patterns that have arisen in the past. It is like an automatic pilot where, based on your experiences in the past, patterns are established for the best way to react in a future situation. According to Daniel Kahneman, a professor and Nobel laureate, this is system 1: the super-fast system that allows you to respond in a fraction of a second without expending too much energy. New insights rarely originate from this system. It allows us to do routine things that we weren't yet able to do when we were born, such as walking, driving, and arriving at our destination in one piece despite heavy traffic. We desperately need this auto-pilot in our unconscious brain, because the billions of decisions and movements we make every day are just too much for our conscious brain. We would crash in complete exhaustion a mere hour after we wake up if we used our conscious brain for these decisions. All new insights arise in our neo-cortex. Kahneman calls this system 2: the slow system. This conscious part of our brain is only activated when it is really necessary, because it uses a considerable amount of energy. It literally burns calories. The quality of our neo-cortex differs per person, as does our consciousness on when we feel the need to use our neo-cortex. Some will find it necessary to use the neo-cortex during work, others during a challenging hobby. Or both, if you've experienced the thrill of how the neo-cortex can enrich your life. It sounds like a paradox, but the use of the neo-cortex is mainly fixed in a routine pattern in the limbic system for all of us.

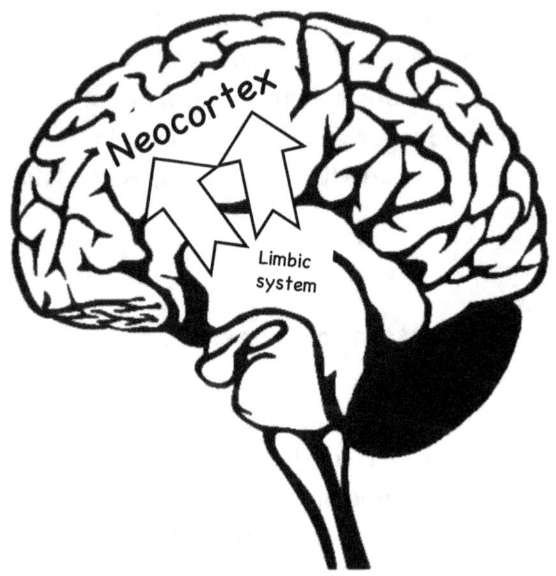

From democracy to sociocracy

A democracy has its pros and cons. The advantage is that everyone has an equal vote, and the right to vote. So, power is not in the hands of an individual, as it would be in an autocracy. And that's fair. It also feels better, and it creates more support. It may seem obvious that democratic decisions are best, and therefore desirable. However, in a holistic systems approach, democracy also has its drawbacks. A democratic outcome is not necessarily the best outcome for the system as a whole. Take a heating system, for example. The thermostat can go to 200 degrees without any problems and the radiators can handle that just fine, so they vote in favor, as it were. The boiler can't handle it, however, so it votes against. When this happens, the system collapses in a democratic way. Another example: a political party that promises to ensure that we no longer have to pay taxes will get many votes. But if this party wins the election based on this promise and actually carries it out, our system of shared facilities would collapse and we would all suffer as a result.

What we need in a system if we want to make the right decisions, is that we listen especially to the minority. We also refer to the minority as 'the outlier'. Listening to the outlier respectfully and without judgment is part of a sociocracy. In a sociocratic process, we deliberately keep perception, opinion formation, and decision-making separate. A group dialogue and decision-making in a sociocracy happen like this:

1. Description of the topic. People start by determining the topic they want to discuss and decide on. This is done without participants expressing their judgment and without attempts to influence other participants.
2. Poker: everyone shows their true colors without being influenced. Everyone makes their opinion explicit, individually and without consultation, for example by writing it on a post-it note. Others should not be able to see this, because this would constitute influencing (framing). Doing this off the top of your head is not an option, because people would adjust their opinion as others express theirs.
3. Everyone shares their opinions. The other participants are not allowed to respond at this stage. This round is about first listening to each other with the utmost respect, and making a sincere effort to understand others.
4. Next, everyone is invited to respond to what others have said. The agile coach makes sure that this is done with arguments and that people play the ball rather than the man. In this round, the aim is not to have discussions, but for participants to listen to each other's reactions to the opinions they heard in the previous round.
5. Now it is time for discussion, with an equal say for all.
6. Direction of resolution or decision. Poker 1: Everyone briefly explains their solution, explicitly but not visible to the others (for example, on a post-it note). Next, everyone takes turns stating what they think is the best solution direction or decision, based on previous rounds. Everyone listens respectfully to the other proposals.

7. Poker 2: Which solution direction do we choose? Pay close attention to the solution the team appears motivated for. Make a proposal to choose the experiment that the team can learn the most from, if opinions are still much divided.

8. Decision based on consent. The solution direction that emerges as the most promising is accepted as an experiment, unless there is an urgent reason the decision may harm the whole or individuals. This means that the decision is given the opportunity to prove itself in practice. If it turns out that in practice the decision does not or insufficiently deliver the intended result, this is followed by another sociocratic round.

Yes, you read that right. There are also elements of democracy and autocracy in this sociocratic decision-making process. After all, in the penultimate step, we consider the majority of the votes, and there is a facilitator or agile coach who makes a proposal. The point is that decisions are made and that it will not be a free for all with endless and indecisive discussions. It is a decision about what the team wants to learn by way of experiment, so we don't have to make it any harder than it is.

From support to awareness

Broad support at the early stages of a change or development process is a fairy tale. Better to start off narrow and deep. Broad support can become a reality only once you become successful. Take sports, for example: the winners have the largest fanbase.

Being successful starts with motivation and energy arising from awareness of the current status and focus on the desired situation.

This is why agile coaches need to start by working on awareness and a sense of purpose, of where one really stands and what is needed to contribute to this. People start moving out of a sense of purpose in an environment that enables this. Why do we do what we do? People who are aware of their pure motives perform significantly better than people who do things because the boss wants them to and because someone will check whether they have done it.

From powering to puzzling

Hierarchical leaders tend to use their power if they want to get something done. If this happens based on the self-righteousness of the leader always knowing best, you are doubly unlucky. Nobody knows best all the time and, in this day and age, more and more things are becoming unpredictable. In the agile organization, we switch off hierarchical power and the ego for a moment; they no longer play a role in how we collaborate. We move from vertical to horizontal thinking. It is not about the power someone has, but about being willing and able to enter into an equal dialogue with everyone. If you are able to connect your neo-cortex with the neo-cortexes of outliers, a solution to the most complex problems is quickly found.

From leading to coaching

Development teams in an agile organization work in self-organization. They are not separate from everything and have no license to go crazy. They focus on the value they have in mind and are given the space to discover for themselves how they can best develop that value. As an agile coach you should never, I repeat, never lead the team. You can teach the team new things, talk to them about best practices, coach them, and facilitate good dialogue sessions, but you can never lead the team. The team should lead itself and decide for itself how they want to work. This approach greatly stimulates creativity and ownership in the team. As a result, agile teams take more responsibility and are motivated to achieve results. Any results are, therefore, the team's and the team's only. There is no boss to tell the team what they should be doing, or how. Everything happens inside the team. That is why a coach is indispensable for teams to gain, and stay in, their strength. This enables them to also perform in self-organization.

Discourage the behavior of team members as well as managers who see you as the leader. Once you fall into this trap, your position as a coach is lost and the path to self-organization is obstructed.

From the comfort zone to the stretch zone

People enjoy being challenged and experiencing that they are growing. That is why the best things do not happen in the comfort zone, where things are predictable and manageable. People become desensitized in their comfort zone because they do not grow and their sense of self-worth diminishes, often resulting in a 'bore-out'. The best learning moments in your life do not come from the 'panic zone' either, where things happen that you cannot handle at all and that you want to block, or flee from. The very best learning moments in your life take place in the

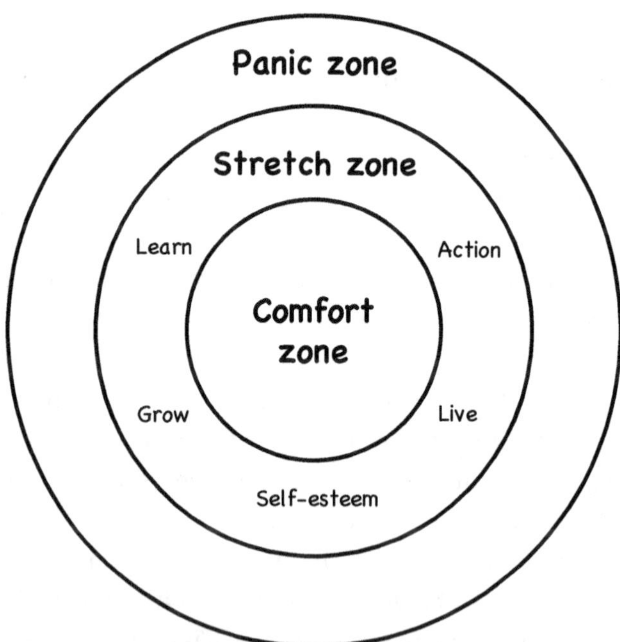

stretch zone, where you are challenged to grow in a way that you can handle. They happen in an environment with people who give you the space and resources to do so.

From tough decisions to light experiments

In traditional organizations, elaborate plans are written and many meetings are held. Decisions are taken by senior management, and they are final. "Stick to the plan" appears to be the motto. This is slow decision-making, which comes with many drawbacks in a mobile environment, such as:

- These kinds of plans and decisions require clairvoyant people who can predict the future.
- These plans are risky because the assumptions have not been validated with real users. As a result, decision-makers try to remove all the innovation, in order to reduce the perceived risk.
- This heavy decision-making hinders the adaptation of plans, because in the same slow decision-making process people have to go past all the decision-makers to get agreement on the adaptations.

The most successful products are successful because they changed into something different from what was originally intended during their development. Wisdom arises along the way, while you are working on it. This makes the case for small and easily adaptable plans. They do not need to be so elaborate and the decision-making is less difficult, because chances are very high that they will be adapted many a time during the course of the process. This is why every decision in an agile organization is an experiment. Whether this is the right decision will become apparent in practice. In an agile organization, this is not left to people who say they can predict the future, but to the facts in practice today (empiricism).

What do you do when you notice that decisions are still being made in a traditional way, and hinder agility? Encourage experiments! Motivate the team to stop demanding big decisions from management. Encourage the team to ask for small budgets for small experiments, explaining that they want to run experiments to prevent plans from failing or wasting time and money. Management will probably not want to ponder this for very long, they will quickly agree. With the outcome of the experiment, the team defines their next assumption based on what they have learned, for which they want to do another small and affordable experiment. This brings the team closer to the moment when management no longer wants to be disturbed for small affordable experiments, and decides to shift the mandate to do this to the team. The experiments result in facts that minimize the risk of failure. Armed with facts and a minimal risk of wasting time and money, decisions also become less burdensome. One fine day, the management will no longer see the value in traditional decision-making based on elaborate predictive plans. From that moment on, the management and teams start working together according to the principle of 'inspect and adapt', in other words: agile.

In addition to motivating the team to take on the competence and mandate while experimenting, the agile coach organizes sessions with the management to explain how agile development delivers the highest value, in the shortest lead time, and with the least risk. Even if not all managers come around immediately, you will have initiated the change on both sides in this way. This is also known as the sandwich method. If you increase the pressure from below and from above simultaneously, anything that is unhealthy will be squeezed out. This will only work if the pressure comes from two sides; it will not happen if the pressure comes from one side only. The agile coach should observe how this process progresses. You have set the sandwich method in motion; the rest is now up to the organization. Inspire as a mentor and mirror as a coach where necessary, but do not lead this process.

From positions to roles

Traditionally, people have had positions that indicate how they are organized in relation to other people, such as commercial director, sales manager, and salesperson. In an agile organization, these kinds of relationships are irrelevant, since work has to be done that leads to value. That is why in an agile organization, roles are preferred over positions. Roles reflect how we organize the work. You could see a role as a collection of activities that have a logical coherence. Having sales conversations with customers is a role. Teaching salespeople new selling skills is a role. And hiring new salespeople is a role as well. Agile coach, product owner, scrum master and team member are also roles, but they do not have any hierarchical relationship to each other. Everyone is in charge of their own role and not of other people's roles.

The roles of an agile coach are, in detail:
- inspiring an agile mindset and working method;
- observing and assessing where the organization and the teams stand in their development toward an agile organization and setting the next step in motion every time;
- sharing knowledge about agile principles and methods;
- delivering the best agile practices and options for experimentation;
- coaching management, teams, and individuals in and around the organization;
- facilitating agile (further) development at the request of the organization, teams, or individuals.

So how do you start to coach the agile organization?

You have to start somewhere, right? Don't sit around and wait until you have ten years of experience before starting, because that would be very difficult in practice. If you don't start, you won't get any experience, and you need experience to be a good agile coach. So, in you jump, at the deep end!

Start small. Don't try to transform a large organization into self-organizing agile teams all in one go. You would be breaking things down, not building.

Find out where in the organization:
- the complexity is greatest;
- the need is greatest;
- the dependence on the rest of the organization is the lowest;
- the possibility exists to work as a start-up outside the premises;
- there is a possibility to develop an end-to-end value chain as a whole in an agile way.

If you can start small in this way and you understand the agile principles, you are already halfway there. And if you have an agile mentor by your side with whom you can share all your ideas and experiences, you will go even faster.

Provide a multidisciplinary team formation with fully available members, preferably not part-timers who also have work and meetings in other teams or departments. Find a product owner who knows the end user's needs, and thus the value for them, well and an experienced scrum master who has no ambition to be a team leader.

Voilà, you have made a start!

So, we bring motivated people together, whom we will motivate even more by getting them to discover in sessions which value they are going to develop and for whom. Needless to say, only after they clearly understand what constitutes value for the end user.

In this way, the product owner will receive plenty of valuable input for his backlog, which he will organize based on the Value-Effort matrix. This creates an explainable development strategy which the product owner uses to enter into a continuous dialogue with the stakeholders.

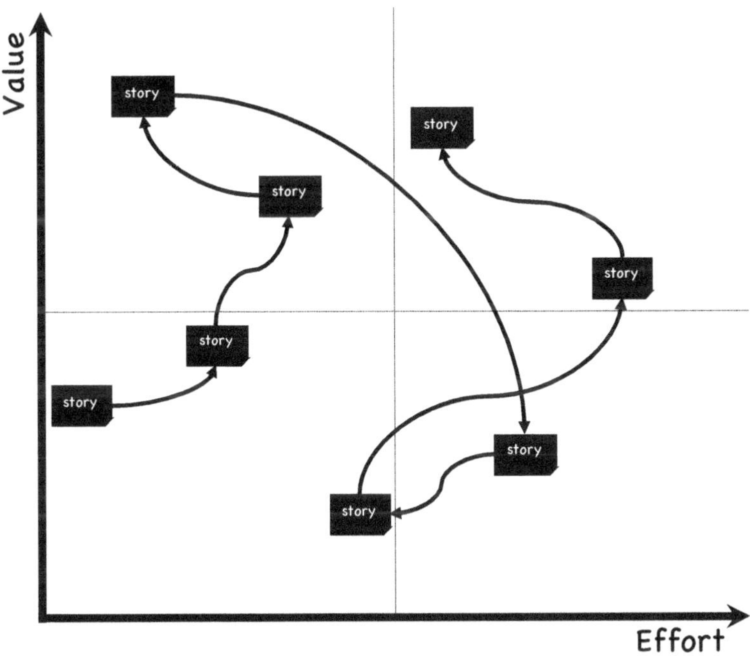

The cycle of continuous improvement can now be organized according to the iterative working method. Sessions are regularly organized at the organizational and team level, to evolve toward the agile organization in a spirit of co-creation.

The organization as a system

Once you have started, you will want people to develop their agile environment as an organic and highly effective system. I often use systems thinking to achieve this.

The word system comes via Latin from the Greek word 'sustema' and literally means 'organic whole'. This also explains the word 'organization'. An organic, living whole, where the elements react to each other in cause-and-effect relationships. These cause-and-effect relationships form unconscious social patterns in the organization, which either strengthen or counteract the organization. Many of the quick fixes that we apply in organizations on a daily basis unintentionally become a counterproductive pattern. They are the side effects of well-intended actions for which you cannot blame anyone because they are no longer able to see the effect of their actions in the organization. As a result, the demand for quick fixes only increases and a downward effect is created, a process which has caused the demise of many organizations. When customers walk away and the internal organization thinks it is because the customers just don't understand or because the competition is cheating, this is a sign that the downward pattern has started. If allegations are made against the administration, management, service department, etc., you should be on high alert because these internal allegations inadvertently make the organization worse. And when the call sounds for a strong leader to teach all the guilty parties a lesson or two, the organization arrives at an advanced stage of an extremely destructive spiral

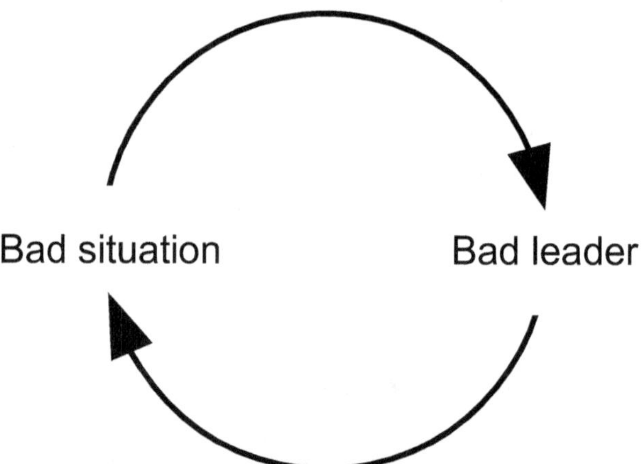

Most people prefer short-term symptom management because they are unable to oversee complex systems. After all, the short term is manageable, and an immediate effect can be observed. In this linear thinking pattern, we encounter problems and solve the problem. Then we run into the same problem again and fix it once more, and so on. However, an organization is a system and not a machine. With a machine you can repair or replace a part, whereas a system is a complex whole with effects and side effects.

Systems thinking makes it easier to make sense of the increasingly complex organic whole (the organization).

As an agile organization coach, you facilitate co-creation sessions in which you visualize the organization as a system around the core variables in a causal loop diagram. This makes the system transparent and understandable. The overview of the organic whole makes people aware of how the system functions in reality. It is an excellent tool for entering into a dialogue. With a shared image of the underlying dynamics that have created the current situation, you will be much better able to design and try out a desired system together. You can learn from this process together, and adjust it every time you think you can improve the system based on experience. In my experience, working in co-creation in this way will always lead to an improved organization.

In systems thinking, you look at the whole instead of at a problem, in other words: a shift in focus from symptoms to structures. This shift starts with the mental model of the people in the organization. What are the prevailing beliefs? Do employees see the organization as a machine, or as an organic system? These are the fundamental beliefs for the organization's culture, which are in turn fundamental to many patterns that would be difficult to break without modifying the mental model. Do the highest-paid people believe that they know a lot, or do they believe that they know little but can learn a lot and in doing so develop the best things? Albert Einstein once said, "The more I learn, the more I realize how much I don't know." This wisdom is also reflected in the Dunning-Kruger effect from 1999, which scientifically demonstrates that people tend to misjudge their abilities. People with below-average abilities tend to overestimate their true abilities, while people with above-average abilities usually do not realize how much better they are. Unfortunately, those with the loudest voices in an organization often have the most confidence within the group with which they interact or work, because they do not realize how incompetent they are and thus come across as confident. Competent people, on the other hand, are more careful about responding quickly and are in a continuous learning mode. Those who don't immediately have an answer to complex questions may well be the smartest Einsteins in the organization. In my experience, the Dunning-Kruger effect regularly has a significant effect on how an organization functions as a system.

When this happens, agile coaches will not create the causal loop diagram of the organization themselves, but instead will do this in collaboration with the people who make up the system. The agile coach takes a curious attitude in this regard and facilitates the development process. This starts with a thorough explanation of why systems thinking with causal loop diagrams can help improve the organization and make it more agile. Next, the process of diverging, converging, and choosing can begin.

1. The participants play poker about what they consider important themes, problems, or issues in the development of an agile organization. Ask everyone present to write a post-it note for each item, without showing anyone else what is on it.

2. The participants come forward one by one and stick each post-it note on the board, explaining to the others what they mean by it. It is important that the participants are not yet allowed to respond to each other's items, not even jokingly. Responding at this stage would impede the free input of ideas. The agile coach observes whether everyone can speak freely and whether everyone's input is listened to respectfully. People are allowed to request clarification, as long as this is not intended to influence opinion formation. Starting with the second participant, everyone adds new items horizontally, and items that have already been mentioned or are similar vertically. This is important information as it shows which items most participants consider important. This is not to say that the item chosen most often is also the most important.

3. Once all the input is on the board, take a step back together with the participants and ask them: "Looking at this, what can we see?" All participants state what they see and everyone respectfully listens to each other's opinions.

4. Then you ask "What is still missing? Would anyone like to add anything?" You will find that people can often think of even more once the context is there. Now anyone who wants to add something can speak up, write down their idea, and add it to the board.

5. Next, we are going to converge, that is, from as much input as possible back to a few important items. Voting by dot helps to speed up this process. You could invite participants to put three dots next to one to three items they consider most important for the success or growth of the agile organization.

6. When the votes are visible, the participants take a step back again and you ask them again: "What are we seeing here?" You will notice that this creates a valuable dialogue, based on which you can properly determine the really important items to tackle now.

7. During the discussions, pay close attention to the variable that seems to be the most important for growth or success. Suggest a single core variable: "If I understand the discussions correctly, am I right in assuming that X is the most important variable for growth or success?" If the group agrees, paste that variable on a blank part of the board. This does not have to be the item with the most votes, but an item which most participants recognize as the most important item for growth or success.

8. Formulate the desired direction in a question and determine the scope, if necessary. For example: we want to be more innovative and the solution has to be budget-neutral.

Now we are ready to visualize what is happening to the core variable in the organization. Otto Scharmer once said: "The essence of systems thinking is to make the system see itself." The goal of the agile coach is to enable a system to see itself.

A causal loop diagram visualizes the relationships between cause and effect. The effect is added with a letter:

1. 'S' for 'same': this is the same causal relationship. For example, if one variable goes up, the other variable also goes up. If you are hungry (cause), the variable of eating (effect) also goes up.

2. 'O' for 'opposite': this is the opposite causal relationship. For example, if one variable goes up, the other variable goes down. The more you eat (cause) the less hungry you are (effect).

3. ǂ (double slash through relation arrow): this double slash alerts us to a relevant or significant time delay in a causal relationship. This effect is like a diesel engine: it takes a while to heat up before this effect starts to work, but once it works, it cannot be stopped. This is important to know, otherwise you may add too much heat because you cannot immediately see the effect, causing the effect to overshoot its target and the diesel engine to catch fire. The value for which you steer is called the setpoint, for example 100 degrees.

   With two slashes through the causal relation line, we know that we have to be alert to this and consider that the effect will need more time to become visible or noticeable. Anyone who has ever driven a boat will probably recognize this. When you turn the rudder, it takes a while before the boat responds. This makes you turn the rudder even more because you don't see the effect. But once the boat starts to turn, you overshoot your aim and before you know it you are lying across the water. This will make you zigzag across the water. When driving a boat, the effect is significantly slower than what we are used to when driving a bicycle or a car.

The effects of the entire feedback loop are also indicated with a letter. These effects can be reinforcing or balancing:

1. 'R' for 'reinforcing': this is a reinforcing effect of a feedback loop in an upward or downward spiral. Start tracing the reinforcing loop as early as possible and keep a close eye on it, because the effect can grow exponentially in both a positive and negative sense (snowball effect). So, if the effect is positive, this is a very valuable loop. If the effect is negative, it is very threatening.

2. 'B' for 'balancing': this loop corrects a variable that deviates from the standard.

The letters and their meaning may take some getting used to at first, so I usually hang up or write a legend to accompany them. This makes the discussion board understandable for everyone, even those who are not familiar with causal loop diagrams (i.e. the majority). The agile coach should make sure everyone understands what it says. It is better to give too much than too little explanation.

3. Ask everyone to play planning poker about what causes a lack of innovation. Ask them to write nouns on separate post-it notes, stick them to the left of the core variable on the board, and explain each one without discussion. After that, everyone is invited to respond and supplement if possible.

4. Now have a poker session about the consequences of the core variable not functioning as desired. Ask them to stick these post-it notes on the board to the right of the core variable. While the participants add the post-it notes, they explain to the other participants what they mean. This is followed by a round of reactions or additions.

5. Ask everyone to go back one step and reflect on what they have created now. My question is usually, "What do you see when you look at this?" Give people room to share the insights with each other. You may be surprised, there will often be insights that had not yet occurred to you!

6. Now have a poker session about the cause-effect relations the participants see. Visualize these closed feedback loops on the board, and ask the participants to consider and respond to them. This process may touch a nerve or two, and the group may throw up the odd accusatory or denying reaction. Be prepared for this to happen. If anyone is looking for a scapegoat, explain immediately that this has no place in this session. "In this session, we only want to discover and understand what is happening in the organization." Or: "Yes but…" responses do not belong in this session. The yield is already very valuable up to this point. Chances are that you have mapped out one or more reinforcing feedback loops, which may or may not overlap. Because the participants did it themselves, the awareness from this session alone will create a better system.

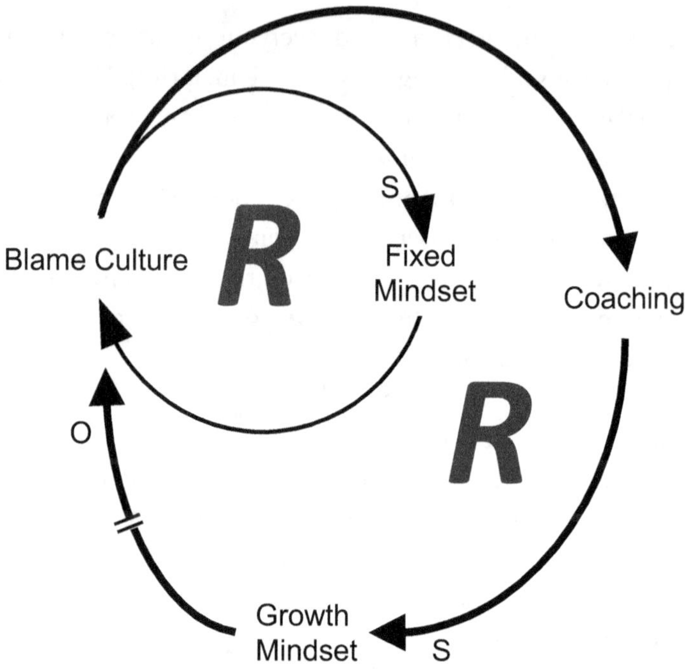

7. Get people to brainstorm about possible healthy systems in groups of two or three for an hour or so. Ask the participants to draw the causal loop diagrams themselves, so that they learn to think in systems. Bring the results together and facilitate a good dialogue. The outcome is likely to be an experiment. Which system will they try out, to learn from?

8. In the next session, evaluate the experiment and possibly go through the same steps to improve the system again with another experiment. Or the team could pick up a new item to improve in the organization.

Development path for the agile organization

Development paths differ for every organization, but in general they all follow this pattern:

1. *Top-down: from awareness to knowing*
Before embarking on a transition from a traditional to an agile organization, it is crucial that the top of the organization knows what an agile organization is, why it is important for their organization, and how a transition proceeds. Organize awareness sessions with the management, followed by sessions with the management, and HR in the presence of the management. Encourage these parties to mutually discuss the need for change.

149

2. *Choose promising areas*
Identify the areas where agile work can quickly show results, such as innovation, product development, marketing, communication, or IT. Go for narrow and deep, so that you can resist the friction that is expected to arise in the organization.

3. *Bottom-up: from awareness to knowing.*
Organize awareness sessions in the workplace of the chosen promising areas. Observe who is most motivated to implement the agile working method, and with whom you might develop an agile unit within the organization.

4. *Set up an iterative learning environment*
Start with the most promising area and the most motivated people. If the most motivated people are not working in the most promising area, start in both areas. The aim is to start up learning environments in the organization that become an example and proof for the rest of the organization.

5. *Invite the environment to attend the reviews and organize Gemba walks*
Invite the managers and employees of the other promising areas to attend the reviews and provide feedback.

Take the opportunity to explain how the team works in an agile way, and demonstrate what has been learned and delivered. The internal evidence has been provided, causing a pull effect. Managers and employees in the other promising areas are mentally in the right lane, as it were, to also adopt the agile mindset and working method as their new way of thinking and acting.

6. *Scaling up*

Once the system is up and running, you examine where you can scale up the fastest. This could be with multiple teams within the same value stream, or with new teams in a new value stream.

Now it is simply a matter of continuously going through the integral coaching model with Wanting, Knowing and Ability, at every layer in the organization. Is it really that simple? It certainly is, in theory! In practice, you can expect to face more challenges.

WHAT WILL YOU ENCOUNTER IN PRACTICE AS AN AGILE COACH?

The client is not familiar with it and wants something else

Your organization has plans for an entirely new value proposition, and you have been asked today to take on the role of agile coach. You had already taken a scrum master course and heard many great stories about successful agile organizations. Moreover, you've just read this book, so you know what the role involves. You want nothing more than to become an agile coach, so you accept enthusiastically. On Monday, the program manager has scheduled a meeting with you to talk about the role. You pick up the Scrum Guide and this book again, to freshen up your knowledge. You also received the Vision Document, the Project Initiation Document (PID) and the Plan of Approach from the program manager. And so you canceled a dinner party this weekend, to give yourself enough time to read these documents carefully. After all, you want to prepare yourself thoroughly for this meeting.

As you read through the documents, a few things jump out at you. The vision document has been drawn up by the management, with the assistance of an external consultancy firm. The content is quite precise, a kind of prediction of the future with finite conclusions. The PID is version 4.8 and deviates from the vision, which may indicate that many adjustments happened before the various MTs were willing to give their approval. The Action Plan is quite extensive, written by the program manager with the help of two internal project managers and an interim manager. The KPIs (Key Performance Indicators) are tightly defined, as are the milestones and release dates. The appendix contains a few more elaborations, including Work Packages and a PowerPoint presentation of 83 impressive slides. The presentation is also included as a compressed PDF file, so that you can easily email it to everyone to inform everyone properly. As you read, you can't help but feel that everything is already set in stone, and you wonder what they need an agile coach for.

On Monday, you arrive in the meeting room mentioned in the email invitation a few minutes before ten, but at five past ten the Program Manager hasn't arrived yet. He sends you a WhatsApp to let you know that he is still at the MT meeting, which is running late. At quarter past ten, he rushes into the room apologetically: "There are some budget issues and there are a few stakeholders in this MT who keep insisting that they want to know in concrete terms what they will be getting, and when. But it worked, I think they will come through. Coffee?" You walk over to the coffee machine together. The program manager wants to make good use of his time, so he immediately starts talking about the content of the program. He wants to deliver the first item next month, to keep the MT on board. Someone told him the agile approach is a quick fix and that you did a course, so that sounded convenient.

You let him talk for a while. Back in the meeting room, the program manager proposes to go through the milestone sheets and the work packages. He has put them in an Excel sheet and suggests putting them on the digital screen. "That's why I chose this room, because it has a nice large screen on the wall, so that we can put all the work sheets and work packages side by side."

This completes your analysis, and you decide an intervention is in order. It's clear that although the program manager and you are both very keen, you probably want different things. And by now, you probably know more about agile than the program manager. As far as the axis of Ability is concerned, the question is whether, armed with your knowledge but with no experience, you will be able to turn this into an agile environment. So, what to do? You don't want to tell him no either, because this is your opportunity to gain experience.

You decide to ask a few in-depth questions: "What is your image of an agile coach?" and "What do you mean by an agile approach?"

Program manager: "You did that scrum course, right? Well, let's get some agile teams together and you just teach them how to scrum, so that they start delivering faster. I have already forwarded the Scrum Guide to the three project managers, because they will be the scrum masters of the teams."

You: "Are you willing to adjust the plan if it turns out in a week that doing this differently will deliver more value?"

The program manager jumps up as if stung: "No, what would we do that for! Do you have any idea how long it took to get all the MTs to agree to this? If we adjust the plan, I will have to go past all those MTs again. It would mean disaster for this project! But you know what, we don't need to change anything, we thought long and hard about it. Let me show you the milestone overview and the release schedule."

You: "It's just a little too early for that. What we now need is for us both to have equal knowledge about the agile way of thinking and acting. Otherwise we risk making the wrong decisions and delaying the project. And we need an agile mentor, who helps us to take the first steps based on practical experience. Do you have time for a knowledge session today? And shall I see if I can find an experienced agile mentor who is available at short notice? Then we can look into how quickly your agile team can deliver tomorrow."

You know that scrum only helps if the environment and the team also think and act in an agile way. Moreover, scrum is not a framework for every type of work, so first of all you want to gather more information about the intended value and the team's room for maneuver.

You: "Why don't we schedule a session for the team? Then we can start building up some knowledge with them, and then I can better assess where they stand."

During this conversation you have observed, as far as possible, what the situation is regarding Wanting, Knowing and Ability. You both Want a fast-delivering unit, you probably Know more about agile, and it is unlikely that you will have the Ability to achieve this in unaltered form. Based on this observation, you chose the right intervention for the time being.

No safe environment

Now the real work starts. How can you create a safe environment in an arena in which managers have made their budgets available and are starting to pull immediately because they want to know if they will get their results? It would not be the first time that the budget holders received an overly rosy project report, following which more budget and time were needed after all, while the value was not delivered. Budget holders also learn from this and don't want this to happen to them again. That is why they ask for more promises, and every orange or red traffic light in the report is cause for a serious conversation. Budgets do not get approved without a struggle, and a kind of price negotiation arises, whether it can be done for less. I recently heard a director say, literally: "Let them prove themselves first! Let's see if they are trying hard enough." Program and project managers can feel the pressure, so they like to keep budget holders at a distance. Team members are not allowed to communicate directly with the MT. From now on, people will speak with one mouth. A steering committee makes the decisions, and all stakeholders require their own reports. Divide and conquer is the winning survival strategy. For the manager to stay out of harm's way, that is. Not for the result.

A safe environment means that everyone can talk openly and freely without the risk of being held accountable. This requires a different type of leadership and accountability, but these are not easy to create. On several occasions, I have been able to get large complex programs that had stalled back on track by asking the management to scrap the steering groups and project management layers for this program. This does not mean that management is now superfluous; they are just given a different role. The management is now going to manage the system rather than the people.

So, as an agile coach, you decide to organize a few knowledge and work sessions for the management that is responsible for the budgets. Once they know more about how to significantly reduce the risk of wasting time and money with an agile approach, this will open up perspectives for an agile approach. For example, budget holders might decide to organize part of the program in an agile way, so that they can discover by experimentation that it does indeed yield better results. Only when they have experienced this, budget holders will be able to let go of their old patterns and adopt agile organizational principles as their new pattern.

The management has no time

You: "To ensure that the teams become more decisive and can deliver faster, I propose that we organize knowledge sessions for the management, so that they know how to make this happen in an agile organization. In addition, I would like team members to no longer be allowed to spend time on progress reports. If a report has to be made at all, someone else should make it without requiring a time effort from team members."

Program manager: "The management doesn't have time for that. And those reports are mandatory. Our teams always make these reports. It's their job, right?"

You: "I understand, but you've seen the results so far, so something will have to change. If the force field stays the same, things will not progress. We have to break through something. Shall we do a retrospective with the teams in a work session? It could teach us a lot. After all, they are the people in the organization who deliver the value. Then we will also do a retrospective with management, so that we can compare it with the team's retrospective. What do you think we might find?"

You are kicking off interesting dialogues that give you the opportunity to look at things in a different way together. The solution usually does not come from one side, such as the management or the teams, but by bringing several sides together.

Seeing is believing

Next, you draw the system. You show how everything and everyone reacts to each other. For example, that poor results generate more demand for reports. And that writing more reports happens at the expense of the time and focus that the team has for delivering results, or vice versa. Having to spend less time on reports and discussions about reports allows the team to spend more time and focus on delivering results, which reduces the need for reports, and so on. You can draw all the critical processes in the system as a causal loop diagram.

You: "Shall we work out where things are currently stagnating? And then work out how we can go in the right direction? Then you'll have a good discussion basis for talking to the budget holders."

The environment does not cooperate

Many organizations have now stopped having individual performance reviews, because it contributes very little to better results for the organization. The functioning of an individual largely depends on the environment in which that person works. For example, bad managers often have employees who function poorly. These employees are then given a poor review, but that review says more about the manager's performance. After all, the manager is responsible for a good working environment.

Desired performance happens in an organization that offers the possibilities to do so. Managers and employees who perform poorly may be able to perform very well in a different environment. And vice versa, of course.

In an agile organization, we put ownership and responsibility back where it belongs, with the person himself or with the agile unit of which one is a part. This requires the ability to introspect (to judge yourself). You also encourage those involved to give each other direct feedback on a horizontal level. After all, horizontal collaboration is crucial to generating value.

If you, as an agile coach, want to help develop an agile environment like this, you will need to engage in an open dialogue with the board and management through work sessions. Preferably do this with the board and the management together in the same session, because the vertical performance pressure here is high and this can stand in the way of changing together. Start with knowledge transfer and practical examples of agile organizations that achieve better results faster, with less risk of wasting time and money. Ask what the participants consider important, and what they want. In this way, create an environment in which the board and management can be coached together.

Next, organize Gemba walks. Gemba comes from the Japanese word 'Genba' and literally means 'the actual place'. In Japan, it means the place where the value is created. A Gemba walk is an invitation to the place where the agile teams work, with the aim of contributing to the value that these teams are developing. Gemba walks are often used to involve the management, for example, but it could also be other stakeholders. Invite them to join the team and give them a tour and explanation on the spot. Ask the product owner to talk about the vision and priorities. And ask the team members to explain what they are doing, what they have learned from real customer behavior, and what they are doing with it.

Instruct the guests in advance about attitude and behavior that is expected during the Gemba walk. They are not supposed to inspect the work to express their judgment on it, nor should they be steering. The goal is that they become familiar with the work of the agile teams and the change that the work entails. A direct dialogue benefits mutual understanding between the team members, which encourages both the team members and the visitors to identify as a holistic unit. It also explicitly requires visitors to think along and contribute to the value creation process. The management and other stakeholders may have different ideas and options than the teams, which can also be valuable. The idea is that the agile teams and the organization are enriched after the Gemba walk, not poorer.

Seeing Agile roles as new titles

So far, so good. The knowledge sessions and retrospectives with the management are behind you. The management is aware of the possibilities and you have been given the opportunity to start small with agile working. The program manager had already appointed one of the budget holders as the product owner, so that he would stay in charge of the whole. He had a busy schedule, however, but he had delegated his mandate to the former department manager who would consult with him for decision-making. To ensure that he will spend enough time on the program, he has scheduled bilateral meetings with the delegated product owner until the end of the year. And the project managers have been appointed scrum masters, so that they can manage the teams properly.

Now it is important that you do not start before the roles have been properly defined. Your first concern is defining the role of product owner. This role requires a heavy customer or user representative: someone who has a clear understanding of the target group, and is at the service of the agile unit that is going to develop the value. The agile unit needs someone to manage the backlog, the stakeholders, and the creation of a shared vision on value and a common goal between the development teams. Product owner is not an honorary title for the person with the highest hierarchical power in the program. Nor is it a duo, steering group, or team. The product owner is a single person who can completely dedicate himself to this role.

It is useful to train, launch, and coach the product owner and the scrum master simultaneously and together. The scrum master will also coach and facilitate the product owner, in addition to the team, in a pure execution of the product owner role. The role of scrum master is not to be the assistant to the team who takes care of everything, or the know-it-all who tells the team what to do. The scrum master is a mini agile coach who is able to focus on the team every day. The scrum master helps the scrum team to apply the scrum rules for agile collaboration as a team, without interfering in the content.

While the product owner creates the initial backlog, you train the team together with the scrum master, help with launching, and coach. Stick to the order of demonstrating, doing together and doing it yourself. One important part of launching the team is that they participate in a session that determines what value the team wants to deliver, and for whom. This is important input for the initial backlog the product owner creates. Wanting, Knowing and Ability apply to all roles. So, first of all, you check whether they want to (encourage with awareness sessions), then you provide the necessary knowledge (training sessions) and then you help them with the launch (mentoring) to achieve sufficient basis to coach them (ability).

The client thinks you are almost done

Many organizations think that agile adoption is done as soon as the knowledge sessions have taken place and you have helped, as a mentor, to launch the agile environment. It is unlikely that all old patterns have already been broken at this stage, however. In other words, the slightest setback will see people falling back into their old world. Knowledge building and mentoring are there to create a playing field in which you can coach. You transition from a proactive to a reactive attitude, which can create the impression that you are no longer needed as much. The checklist is complete, so everyone is now familiar with it, right? Correct, but the goal of knowing is ability. Knowing alone will not get you there, this is where your coaching role begins. Observe where the team currently is and identify where the best opportunity lies for the next step in the team's development. Your role as a teacher and mentor will need to take a backseat for now. Now it's the team's turn to pick up the thread and bring about their own progress. You can encourage this process by asking the right in-depth or powerful questions, based on observation. Preferably address the entire team and not the persons in the team individually, as it is important that progress comes from the team dynamics.

To activate the team to find solutions, preferably ask non-judgmental, open questions. These are also known as ignorant questions and start with: what, who, where, what, as a result of what, when, or how. There is an open question that coaches prefer not to ask, which the 'why' question. Asking 'why' may come across as being called to account. People are unconsciously inclined to defend themselves when being asked 'why', which means you would miss out on the open dialogue that you want to create. If you are still eager to know why something is what it is, start the question with "what", such as, "What makes you handle this in this way?" This avoids evoking the 'accountability pattern' in the brain, but does encourage the dialogue about what caused a person to do something.

Another tip for effective dialogues is to inform from the outside in: don't go straight to the core of the matter, but try to get more information about the context first. This creates a better dialogue structure and yields much more information eventually.

You could start by showing interest in the environment or the situation: "What do you encounter?" or "What are you up against?" This will give you a better feel for the context, allowing you to better interpret the information that follows. Next, show genuine interest in the behavior: "What did you do next?" or "What are you going to do with that?" Now the context is complete. You know what the situation is, and what action goes with it. Now we move on to the skills and beliefs: "What can you do about this?" and "What do you believe in?" or "What do you think is the real solution?" And finally, you arrive at the core of the matter: "What is the most valuable solution for the users and the organization?"

The management thinks your services are no longer needed

The first successes have been scored. The teams feel good about themselves and the management has expressed their admiration for the teams and praised their performance. Everyone appears to be in a good flow.

However, every team inevitably gets to the unconscious-incompetent phase, including successful mature teams. Agile coaching knows no end. Anyone who wants to continuously improve themselves has a coach, including the agile coach. The involvement of the same agile coach does have a sell-by date. You may feel that you are so familiar with the environment that another agile coach could never replace this. However, open-mindedness and objectivity may diminish over time and this can become an issue. Of course, this all depends entirely on how intensely you are involved in an organization, but after three years or so the time has usually come to take the initiative yourself and introduce a new agile coach. The new coach brings an entirely level-headed view of where the teams and the environment are at that moment, and probably sees new opportunities for growth from this moment on.

The client expects you to immediately make many forceful interventions

Fortunately, you paid attention to the development process for agile teams during the knowledge sessions for higher management. As a result, you are able to visualize when the intervention of the agile coach is effective and when it is not.

Once you are in the coaching phase, it is important not to intervene too quickly. The board, the management, and the teams learn to manage their own improvements; give them the space they need to do so, in order to encourage this agile principle as a good habit. Stay away from anything they try out for themselves to learn from. Making them aware that they are learning and that their autonomy is growing is sufficient. Pay close attention, and observe how the system works. If this learning and growth process is not progressing well, it is time to start asking non-judgmental questions. Do this mainly at times when the entire team is together. For example, "When was your last retrospective?" and "What are your experiences with retrospectives?" This will give you an idea of the context. Chances are that you can already read between the lines how the team is experiencing the learning and growth process. Next, ask about the core of the matter: "Which things are often brought up in the retrospectives?" and "How do you come up with improvement experiments?" or "How quickly do you perform the improvement experiments?" If the learning and growth process is organized according to the agile principles, the team will regularly conduct retrospective sessions specifically designed for this. If you suspect that this is not going well, but the team tells you that the retrospectives are going well, continue with something along the lines of "What is the last improvement experiment you implemented?", "What was the result?", "How satisfied are you about this?" and the action question "What could be the next improvement for you?" Please make sure you don't hold them to account. The aim is to have a constructive dialogue, in which the team can discover independently how to improve itself. If the team asks for suggestions, you can make suggestions from your mentor role. If this is not necessary, avoid disturbing their learning process, but reinforce it by giving them space. In other words, decide to do nothing for now, but continue to observe!

Survey as an empirical research method

Saying something is not the same as actually doing something. Paul Postma wrote a fun booklet about this: Sensible Thoughts and Infantile Actions. Therefore, do not rely on what people say, but observe what is actually happening. Sure, this will take more time than just asking what is going on, but trust me, it's worth it. It's better to spend more time observing than to spend little time and be misled. People often give a rational and socially desirable answer, which makes things easier, and there is no need to discuss it. Our reluctance to enter into discussion unless we absolutely need to, is a real imperfection in our brains. If we can avoid discussions, we will do so almost automatically. Most people don't feel like having a discussion, unless they expect it to be beneficial.

Suppose you asked people if they ever throw garbage on the street. Chances are that almost everyone will say they don't. But the situation on the street paints a different picture. There is garbage everywhere, and someone must have left it there. Maybe your assumption is that teenagers are responsible for the garbage. If you really want to find out, however, you hide behind the bushes to observe a spot where there is litter on the street. You may find that in actual fact, it's old people with Zimmer frames. Talk to them in order to develop real solutions.

Observing and learning with small experiments is better than starting a major educational campaign for all teenagers based on an assumption, only to find out that the garbage is still there afterwards. Choose small experiments that cost little and that you can do quickly.

Use the same principle to develop the organization. An employee satisfaction survey in the form of a questionnaire provides, at most, a platform where people can express their frustrations anonymously. It is an indication that there is room for improvement. But before you know it, you will be fighting symptoms. Here too, enter into a dialogue and learn from small experiments how to organize things better.

The management continues to request reports

You can see that the management finds it difficult to break their old habits. They continue to look for ways to direct 'their' employees and to build in control mechanisms to see whether employees are doing what the management has instructed them to do. There is leverage in this. As long as the management has no confidence in the teams, it will ask for reports. The management needs to see:
- what is going on in the organization;
- whether things are improving;
- whether the time is well spent;
- whether no budget is wasted;
- whether the intended results are achieved.

In an agile environment, we always work in complete visibility and we show what we are doing eagerly and often, through rich dialogues with relevant individuals or groups. In agile team rooms, everything is always displayed on the wall, and remote agile teams use real-time online whiteboards. This is how agile teams report, supplemented with a direct dialogue between the makers and the stakeholders. This is much more effective than a static snapshot in a report that is passed on via a manager, and of which the makers are informed via the same intermediary whether the report gives cause for adjustment. In other words, intensively involve the management that requests reports in the teams' practical work and progress. Once this mechanism meets the management's needs, the need for traditional static reporting through management will start to diminish.

After the initial successes, the teams revert to old behaviors

The agile organization is based on working with motivated people. To achieve this, we use Daniel Pink's theory, as described earlier. And if along the way we notice motivation dropping off, or when new people join the unit, don't forget to organize awareness sessions again, followed by knowledge building. I have experienced that people thought that this was only necessary at the start and that anyone joining later would simply fall into step. However, the reality is different, and this is unfair to new arrivals. They deserve a fair chance to a proper entrance; the first blow is half the battle applies here, too.

The team can't see it anymore

Anything that the team cannot solve by itself, but where, according to your estimate, a next step for improvement is possible, should be discussed in a team session. Your aim is for the team to handle this by itself. In many cases, the team session is therefore a retrospective, focused on a specific goal. For example, improving team spirit, or backlog management. The Forcefield Analysis method is often highly effectively here. See the image below for the canvas. The team members then have a poker session to gain insight into the force field.

- They start with the right-hand side and indicate in three, four or five gradations what contributes to improving the chosen item.
- Next, they also show on the left-hand side, in three, four, or five gradations, what causes the item to deteriorate.

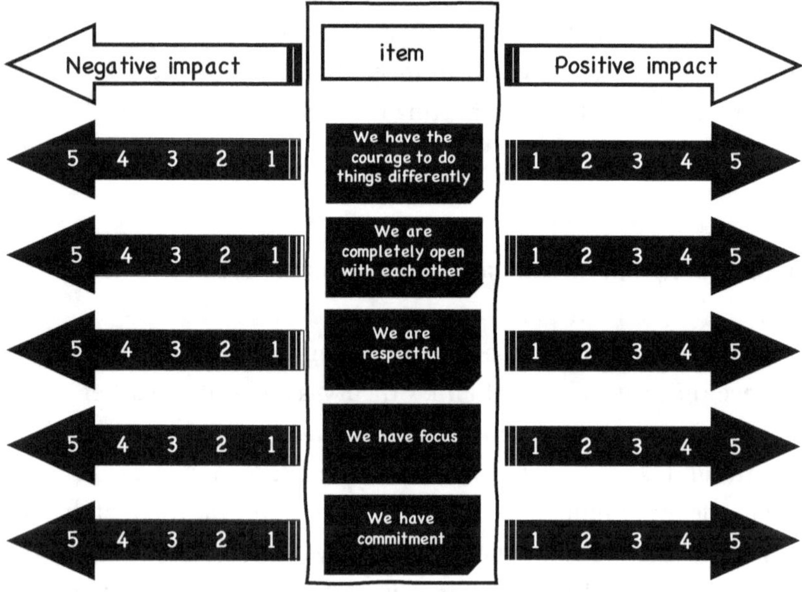

You don't need to feed them anything, because the participants can easily indicate this with many examples. All you have to do is facilitate the group dialogue, to create a collective picture of how they can improve themselves. I use Forcefield Analysis a little differently than the original theory intended (see example below), because I have experienced that my participants understand it more quickly in this way.

The team fails to come up with solutions

Only when the retrospective does not resolve an issue and a team session in which the team takes the lead does not work, does the agile coach step in with a hard intervention. The agile coach puts the problem in the middle of the table and states that it must be solved. The agile coach could also make concrete solution proposals here, on an organizational or team level, preferably in that order. Using causal loop diagrams, analyze the barriers and ask for experiments that might lead to solutions. If this does not yield a solution, you can be all but certain that the right people are not on board. By people, we mean:

1. the agile coach;
2. the people who run the organization;
3. the team members.

You have worked on awareness, insight and knowledge. The management and the team have been helped on their way with mentoring and coaching in three layers. And they have been unable to achieve an agile way of growing. Change the agile coach to exclude the relationship between coach and organization/team as the culprit. If things get better after that, there is your solution. If not, a change of people in the organization is a plausible option. And if all else fails, a change of team composition could lead to a solution. Doing nothing is not an option, because organizations and teams that fail to grow in their agile working methods are slowly but surely dying.

TOOLBOX FOR THE AGILE COACH

What is inside your toolbox as standard? The answer is short: everything you need to facilitate good dialogues. In any case, you always carry post-it notes and markers, because you want to be able to have a clear and structured dialogue with everyone. For the post-it notes, I always choose Super-Stickies by 3M and Neuland markers. The latter are water-based; this is better for the environment and they don't smell or leak. Moreover, they are refillable, so also sustainable in that respect.

If you have online contact, preferably do so using a real-time video connection, so that you can see each other. Non-verbal communication always says more than just verbal communication. You could use Skype, MS Teams, Zoom, or Webex. Zoom is my favorite, because you can easily use breakout rooms. You should also be proficient with online whiteboards. MS Teams and Zoom offer these, albeit with limited functionality. The whiteboards on, for example, Mural, Miro, or Jamboard are even better.

For online sessions, make sure you use the largest screen you can afford. For an agile coach, the ability to perceive non-verbal signals is crucial. If you use a separate microphone that only records sound from the front, there is no need to wear headphones or earphones. Position the microphone in front of your speakers and turn the speakers so that the sound faces away from you. This avoids surface noise and feedback, making things more comfortable.

Needless to say, your smartphone has a timer that allows you to monitor the time during work sessions. Physical or online timers are even better:

you can show them on a digital screen, so that participants can see how time passes. Miro also offers a timer that the participants see on their whiteboard. And you give teams a physical ELMO stuffed toy, that they can use when they feel there's too much talking and not enough action (Enough, Let's Move On).

In addition, you have plenty of methods and games in your toolbox, which you can deploy at any time. This is often what distinguishes one agile coach from the next. The trick is to facilitate the right dialogues your way, to arrive at the right insights and changes that add value. There are four main categories of working methods:

1. diverge: collect as much relevant information as possible
2. order: relative weighting for overview and insight, for example, based on two extremes
3. converge: bring a plethora of information back into focus based on the most important information
4. decision-making: so that we always keep going and never stand still

You can find many useful methods in several books and on websites that have been devoted to this topic, such as Gamestorming and Innovation-games, or tastycupcakes.org and teamretro.com.

If you are not a good agile coach yourself and you don't think you will become one, how do you find one?

Anyone can call themselves an agile coach; it is not a protected profession. As a result, there are many pseudo agile coaches, such as former waterfall project managers who nowadays sell their services as agile coaches. There is much less demand for waterfall project managers these days, and agile coaches are in high demand. If you follow the money, you end up with a slew of pseudo agile coaches.

Now I have nothing against former waterfall project managers; I know several who have completed a successful transition to a fertile agile mindset. They have experienced the frustration the waterfall approach entails in a rapidly changing environment. So, they have experienced in practice how not to do it, and based on that frustration discovered how it can be done. I also know former waterfall project managers, however, who continue to believe in their old values and have simply put on a new hat.

My point is, carefully consider people's ideas on developing new value. Ask what value means to them and test whether the agile beliefs as described in this book match your candidate. For example, if someone wants to dogmatically impose the rules of scrum on a team, you are most likely dealing with a wolf in sheep's clothing. Explain that you are not looking for an executive scrum teacher and politely tell them goodbye. It is better to spend a little more time searching now than to fall into a trap that will greatly disadvantage you later on. These pseudo agile coaches can cause much destruction and cast a slur on the mental legacy of agile thinking, which will not be easy to remedy. A successful agile transition is based on trust. And trust arrives on foot but leaves on horseback.

AFTERWORD

Needless to say, I would never have been able to write this book if I hadn't had the opportunity to experiment and learn a lot in the past ten years. This book is just one of the results, and I am merely its collector, editor, and transmitter. I am part of a holistic whole of worlds, cultures, organizations, teams, entrepreneurs, agilists, boards, managers, trainers, consultants, authors, speakers, family, family members, friends, and acquaintances. This includes even the people who are sitting next to me as I write this on a sunny terrace with a beautiful view of De Cannenburgh Castle in Vaassen. It sounds like they are entrepreneurs who are sharing their beliefs. I am learning from them, too, just as I am learning from the castle and its history. In fact, I am deeply indebted to the entire world in which I live. So, allow me to take a deep bow: thank you world, for allowing me to learn and grow indefinitely!

I don't expect that a long list of names here would add much to the value that readers experience in this book. So, although my family, my publisher, and my clients have contributed significantly, I will not bore my readers with all their names. I will limit myself to a small selection of special people who have contributed significantly to the book you see before you. I want to mention my fellow agile coaches Gert-Jan Danenberg, Roland Flemm, Ahmed Sidky, Martijn van Asseldonk, and Anton Vanhoucke. They have invested some of their valuable time in reviewing the content of this book and providing me with sharp and unvarnished feedback. This has undoubtedly benefited this book, which is very valuable for you, the reader. I consider Wieke Oosthoek and Fleur Goppel my mentors in writing this book. This book is an amalgamation of their experience in writing good books and my experience as an agile coach. This has also provided value for the readers. Thank you all very much for this!

References to sources of inspiration

Like most authors, I did not come up with much of the wisdom and substantiation in this book all by myself, let alone that I scientifically demonstrated it. It is the result of a collection of sources that inspired me and stimulated me to experiment in practice. This has yielded plenty of practical experience for me in recent decades, which I have tried to trace back to its scientific basis or other useful sources in this book as much as possible. This definitely includes the following sources. I hope that they will also inspire you to deepen yourself and further shape your experiments in practice.

Adkins, L. (2010). *Coaching Agile Teams*. Publisher Addison-Wesley Professional.

Argyris, C., Schön, D. (1978). *Organizational Learning: a Theory of Action Perspective*, Publisher Addison-Wesley.

Bakker, A., & Halmans, J. (2016). *Coachen met LEF* (2de druk). Boom Publishers Amsterdam.

Booth Sweeney, L., Meadows, D. (1995–2010). *The Systems Thinking Playbook*, Chelsea Green Publishing.

Brugman, K., Budde, J., Collewijn, B. (2010). *Ik (k)en mijn ikken*, Publisher Thema.

Brugman, K., Budde, J. (2016). *Coachen met The Voice Dialog*, Publisher Thema.

Bryan, B., Goodman, M., & Schaveling, J. (2018). *Systeemdenken – Van goed bedoeld naar goed gedaan* (2de druk). Boom Publishers Amsterdam.

Coleman, D. (2004). *Emotionele Intelligentie*. Publisher Olympus.

Denning, S. (2011). *'The Reinvention of Management'*, Strategy & Leadership, Vol 39. No. 2.

Drake, N. (2018) publication in National Geografic magazine, National Geographic.

Edmondson, A. (2014). *Building a psychologically safe workplace,* TEDxHGSE.

Hoogveld, M. (2016). *Agile Managen,* Publisher Van Duuren Management.

ICAgile (2020). *Learning Roadmap Agile Coaching Track Version 2.0,* International Consortium for Agile.

Jeanne Liedtka, J., Ogilvie, T. (2011). *Designing for Growth: A Design Thinking Tool Kit for Managers,* Columbia University Press.

Kat, N. (2016). *Coachen met een leeg hoofd* (6de druk). Publisher Van Duuren Management. Labs.spotify.com/2014/09/16/squad-health-check-model/

Laloux, F., Parker, N. (2014). *Reinventing Organizations,* own publishing.

Lencioni, P., (2002). *The Five Dysfunctions of a Team,* Publisher John Wiley & Sons Inc.

Lencioni, P., (2005). *Overcoming the Five Dysfunctions of a Team,* Publisher Jossey- Bass. Managementimpact.nl/artikel/wat-leren-7-stappen-van-googles-high-performance-teams/

Osterwalder, A., Pigneur, Y. (2009). *Business Model Generatie,* Publisher Kluwer.

Pink, D. (2010). *Drive! – de verrassende waarheid over wat ons motiveert.* Publisher Business Contact.

Pol, van der, G.M. (2016). *Coachen als professie* (4de druk). Boom Publishers Amsterdam.

Ramos, C. (2014). *Emergent,* CreateSpace Independent Publishing Platform.

Robertsen, B. (2016). *Holacracy,* Publisher Business Contact, second edition.

Rosenzweig, Ph. (2007). *Het HALO-effect,* Publisher Business Contact.

Scharmer, O. (2017). *Theorie U,* fifth edition, Publisher Christofoor

Schaveling, J. en Bryan, B. (2015). *Systeemdenken voor managers – Wijs omgaan met onze organisaties.* Publisher Academic Service.

Sutherland, J., Swaber, K. (2017). *The Scrum Guide,* Scrum.Org and ScrumInc.

Spanjersberg, M., Hoek, van den, A. Veldhuijzen van Zanten, E. en Wingerden, van, R. (2016). *Systeemdenken in de praktijk – De kunst van het verbinden* (second edition). Publisher Stili Novi.

Takeuchi, H., Nonaka, I. (1986). *The New New Product Development Game,* Article in Harvard Business Review.

Tijsse Klasen, I., Stam, J.J. en Tijsse Klasen, F. (2020). *Slimmer met het systeem – Een nieuw perspectief op complexe organisatievraagstukken*, Publisher Het Noorderlicht.

Vroemen, M. (2010). *Management executive, Teamwerk moet vaker dan het hoeft*, Kluwer Management.

Walthuis, K. (2014). *Wisselende contacten, de ontmaskering van de coachrelatie* (third edition). Scriptum Psychologie.

Wodtke, Ch. (2016). *Radical Focus*, own publishing.